Amílcar Cabral

A POLITICAL LIFE IN MOTION

MÁRIO DE ANDRADE

Published in April 2024 by
1804 Books, New York, NY

1804Books.com

ISBN: 979-8-9882602-7-1
Library of Congress Control Number: 2024936686

Amílcar Cabral—A Political Life in Motion
Edição da Fundação Amílcar Cabral
© Fundação Amílcar Cabral, 2014
Organized by: Luís Fonseca, Olívio Pires, and Rolando Martins
Pagination: Burótica de S. Vicente, Lda.
Printing and finishing: Praia, 2014

Mário de Andrade
Translated by Fraser Robinson and edited by Desmond Fonseca

Cover by Kael Abello and Vivek Venkatraman

Table of Contents

Appendices

Foreword to the English Edition

Among the numerous authors who have studied and written about the life and work of Amílcar Cabral, Mário de Andrade enjoyed a singularly privileged position. The long stretches of the journey that he took together with Cabral in the struggle to dismantle, combat, and defeat Portuguese colonialism generated great emotional closeness, a convergence of visions, and complicity in action. In addition to all this, it is important to mention Andrade's recognized intellectual authority as an author and researcher.

Mário Pinto de Andrade (1928–90) occupies a leading place in the contemporary history of Angola and the national liberation movements of the Portuguese colonies. At the same time, he was one of the most prominent and influential African personalities of the twentieth century, particularly in the spheres of politics, literature, and the social sciences.

The founder and first president of the People's Movement for the Liberation of Angola (MPLA)—the most successful of the three Angolan movements that led the armed struggle against Portuguese colonialism in Angola and the party responsible for proclaiming Angolan independence in 1975—Mário de Andrade was one of the main architects of the unitary action of the liberation movements of the Portuguese colonies in Africa. He participated in the creation and leadership of the organizations created for this purpose—the Anti-Colonial Movement (MAC), the African Revolutionary Front for the Independence of Portuguese Colonies (FRAIN), and the Conference of Nationalist Organizations of the Portuguese Colonies (CONCP)—in close coordination with Amílcar Cabral and other nationalist leaders.

An intellectual, deeply committed to the causes of the emancipation of African peoples, Andrade was the editor for many years of the journal *Présence Africaine*, a key publication on the history of Black-African thought in the twentieth century that had been founded by Alioune Diope and published in Paris. He was also one of the organizers of the First Congress of Black Writers and Artists held in Paris in 1956, of which he was also the secretary. He was close to such personalities as Nicolas Guillén, Léopold Sédar Senghor, Aimé Césaire, Jean-Paul Sartre, Frantz Fanon, René Depestre, and François Maspero, among others.

As both a sociologist and writer, his legacy includes a rich and varied body of work, including anthologies of poetry and Black literature in Portuguese, as well as important literature on the national liberation struggles of Angola and Guinea-Bissau. One of his areas of research that has received the most attention concerned the deeds and ideas of Amílcar Cabral, to which he devoted several works, including the dissertation for his doctoral thesis entitled *La pensée politique d'Amílcar Cabral—genèse et développement*.

A strong friendship linked the two since their student days in Lisbon and was reinforced over time in the struggles that united them against their common enemy, Portuguese colonialism. In an interview with writer Michel Laban, Andrade recalled the impression that Cabral made on him when they first met in Lisbon: "From this first handshake, from this exchange of words, I retained a strong, very pleasant, and very intense impression of having immediately found a friend and immediately being on the same wavelength, so to speak."

From this meeting onwards, Andrade and Cabral's paths became increasingly intertwined: they were involved in the creation of the Center for African Studies, in the political tumult at the Casa dos Estudantes do Império, and in the mobilization and consciousness-raising of Africans living in Portugal. Together with some brilliant young intellectuals from the Portuguese colonies such as Agostinho Neto, Marcelino dos Santos, Eduardo Mondlane, and other nationalists, they were at the root of the strategy of creating a common front of national liberation movements in the fight against Portuguese colonialism, which was successively embodied in MAC, FRAIM, and CONCP. These organizations also played an important role in mobilizing international support for this struggle. These young nationalists, whom Mário de Andrade would later describe as "Cabral's generation," "to refer to the most illustrious of us . . . ," demolished the civilizational myths that constituted the ideological basis of the centuries-old oppression exercised over colonial peoples, challenged repressive power, organized resistance, and liberated their countries, bringing down an empire that considered itself to be eternal.

Amílcar Cabral—Essai de biographie politique was published in 1980 by Librairie François Maspero, in Paris. The following year, the Mexico City publisher Siglo Veintiuno published its version in Spanish with the title *Amílcar Cabral—Ensayo de Biografía Política*.

The French edition continued Andrade's long-standing collaboration with Maspero, which had already published the collections of texts by Amílcar Cabral that he had compiled: *Guinée "portugaise": le pouvoir des armes* (1970); and *Unité et lutte* in two volumes, *L'arme de la théorie* and *La pratique révolutionnaire* (1975); as well as two titles written by Andrade himself about Angola's national liberation struggle, *Liberté pour l'Angola* (1962) and *La guerre en Angola, Étude socio-économique* (1971).

Once the French edition was published, Andrade, who as a tribute to Cabral's memory had accepted the invitation of the young Republic of Guinea-Bissau to take on the role of Minister of Information and Culture, was working on the version to be published in Portuguese when Nino Vieira's coup d'etat overthrew the government he was part of, inaugurating the long period of political instability that continues in Guinea-Bissau to this day. Refusing to compromise with the coup plotters, Andrade had to leave the country that had fraternally welcomed him and in whose project of revolutionary transformation inspired by Cabral's vision he had enthusiastically committed to in the field of culture, with notable results.

This dramatic event, which among other consequences put an end to the project of unity between Guinea-Bissau and Cape Verde—which had been one of Amílcar Cabral's main objectives—as well as the convulsions that resulted from it, led Mário de Andrade to change his plans for the publication of his book, which closes with a chapter on the current state of Cabral's thinking on a positive note, confident that *"followers of the work of Amílcar Cabral"* would be carrying out their political testament on the path of building *"balanced, endogenous development, within the framework of a national and revolution-*

ary democracy which will characterize the future State of the Union of Republics in Guinea-Bissau and Cape Verde."

The coup d'etat carried out by Cabral's former companions and their open questioning of his legacy necessarily led Andrade—himself a direct victim of the coup—to hesitate to publish his work in Portuguese.

In handwritten notes on correspondence held in his estate, Mário de Andrade reveals that he intended to enrich the Portuguese version he planned to publish with new reflections prompted by the coup, intending in particular, *"interpret more broadly (. . .) a very enlightening and useful document for understanding the 'sociology' of the coup d'etat in Guinea-Bissau: 'For the reorganization of the People's Revolutionary Armed Forces,'"* a document where, already in the original in French, he devotes great attention to the interpretation of Cabral's approach to misconduct by some PAIGC fighters. He also planned to add an afterword where, still in the light of the coup d'etat, he would "question Cabral's theoretical corpus, the PAIGC's political practice, in approaching and solving the triple problem of national independence, Guinea/Cape Verde unity, revolutionary national democracy," as well as "discuss the "historical responsibility" of the African petty bourgeoisie and its <u>overdetermined</u> (*sur-déterminé*) role in relation to the peasantry and the proletariat. Unfortunately, his health condition in the following years prevented him from carrying out his plans, and he passed away in 1990, leaving only the manuscript of the book in Portuguese to which (probably before the coup) he had added some additional notes, small additions, and improvements relative to the French version.

This is the text that the Amílcar Cabral Foundation published in 2014 and whose translation is now presented by 1804 Books to North American readers.

This "biographical essay" constitutes the first systematized work on the life path, thoughts, and work of the giant of twentieth-century African history that was Amílcar Cabral, tragically murdered on the eve of the realization of one of his most ardent dreams, the independence of Guinea-Bissau and Cape Verde.*

---

*   It should be noted that in 1975 Izdatel'stvo Politicheskoy Literatury (Political Literature Publishing House) in Moscow published *Amílkar Kabral—syn Afriki* [*Amílcar Cabral—Son of Africa*] by Soviet journalist Oleg Ignatiev, later published in Portuguese by Edições Progresso, also of Moscow. Despite the fact that it was a worthy and well-intentioned effort intended to honor Cabral and make him known to Soviet public opinion, it ended up being a romanticized work containing many factual inaccuracies. — Luis Fonseca

Benefiting from his privileged proximity to Cabral which enabled him to directly witness Cabral's role in the "major steps that marked [his] life," Mário de Andrade is the perfect person to guide us in exploring the paths taken by the founder and leader of PAIGC in a process in which action and reflection illuminate each other. Mário de Andrade did not intend to use this work to present a complete biography of Amílcar Cabral (he qualifies his own work as a "biographical sketch"), instead, he proposed, based on an analysis of Cabral's intellectual production "to reconstitute [. . .] the political and intellectual itinerary of the PAIGC leader." The book's subtitle *Essai de biographie politique* should be understood in this context.

In fact, in a review of Patrick Chabal's book *Amílcar Cabral: Revolutionary Leadership and People's War*, Mário de Andrade writes that: "Ultimately, it is not easy, in the current state of knowledge, to write a complete biography of Amílcar Cabral, a multifaceted personality who was an agricultural engineer, theorist, politician, military leader, and diplomat. An overall understanding of the man, and of the people's war of which he was the main architect, will have to be based on a vast set of sources that will have to be deciphered [. . .]"

In the introduction to his work, Mário de Andrade entrusts the "historians of the future" with the task of dealing in depth with the multiple facets of Cabral's contributions to a range of domains of knowledge.

More than four decades later, we see that many authors have taken up the challenge. Examples include the important contributions of those who lived or interacted with the Guinean-Cape Verdean leader, such as Basil Davidson, Gérard Chaliand, Óscar Oramas, Lars Rudebeck, Immanuel Wallerstein, François Houtart, Ronald Chilcote, and the plethora of writers and academics from successive generations who have written biographies about him (the aforementioned Patrick Chabal, Julião Soares de Sousa, António Tomás, Peter Karibe Mendy, and others), or who have focused on specific aspects of his action and the ideas produced in its context.

This work by Mário de Andrade can be considered a classic in the historiography of the national liberation struggles of the Portuguese colonies. It is the subject of numerous references and citations in works, articles, and dissertations on anticolonial resistance in Africa by authors from various continents. Forty-four years after its first publication in French, *Amílcar Cabral—Essai de biographie politique* remains one of the main sources of knowledge on the genesis and evolution of Amílcar Cabral's theoretical production. It is therefore appropriate that in the year in which we are celebrating the centenary of his birth, it will finally be made available to English speakers, with this welcome initiative from 1804 Books.

— Luís Fonseca
Chair
General Council of the Amílcar Cabral Foundation

Foreword to the Cape Verdean Edition

In 1980, for the first time (and in French) the French publishing house Maspero published *Amílcar Cabral—Essai de biographie politique* by Angolan writer Mário Pinto de Andrade, at the time a prominent figure in African nationalism and a well-known political and literary essayist. Subsequently, Andrade dedicated himself to preparing a Portuguese version, which, unfortunately, he was unable to see published before his death in 1990. Thus, he bequeathed the manuscript to posterity.

Within the scope of its aim of disseminating the thought and work of its namesake, the Amílcar Cabral Foundation now has the honor of marking the ninetieth anniversary of the birth of Amílcar Cabral with the publication of the Portuguese version of Andrade's *Essai de biographie politique*.

It should be noted that Mário de Andrade, himself a prominent figure of the generation in the vanguard of the movement that would lead the Portuguese colonies to independence, is undoubtedly the individual best placed to observe the genesis of Amílcar Cabral's thought during the various phases of the liberation struggle.

Since Cabral and Andrade's time in Lisbon, when a group of students from the then Portuguese colonies created the Centro de Estudos Africanos with a view to rediscovering their African roots and preparing for their return to their respective countries of origin, to the period that followed the formation and consolidation of the bases of the liberation movements and the transition to "direct action" or "criticism of arms," Mário de Andrade and Amílcar Cabral were always *compagnons de route* and frequently worked together to prepare and present political positions to international organizations and the public in various countries.

They were also the main drivers of the Movimento Anti-Colonialista [Anti-Colonial Movement (MAC)], whose Manifesto inspired the birth of the resistance to Portuguese colonial domination and the creation of CONCP, a unified platform for independence movements in the Portuguese colonies.

In this essay, Mário de Andrade seeks to reconstruct Amílcar Cabral's political and intellectual journey, to show the lines of force and the bonds of agreement in his thought and action, which achieve a perfect dialectical synthesis in his person, and to highlight the original aspects of his theoretical contribution as the leader of a revolutionary struggle for national liberation.

In elegant and confident prose, Mário de Andrade's detailed analysis of Amílcar Cabral's thought seeks to locate the entirety of his intellectual production and praxis within the historical context in which it developed. To this end, he considers the positive influences on Cabral, as well as why and how things happened—which sometimes involves remembering what some may wish to forget.

The *Essai* is divided into four parts: "Part I—The Emergence of the Unifier"; "Part II—The Weapon of Criticism and the Instruments of Knowledge"; "III—Sociology of the People's War"; "IV—Theoretical Contribution"; "Conclusion." In general terms, the sections contain several chapters; as a whole, they correspond to the various stages taken by Amílcar Cabral on the long and difficult journey towards the independence of Guinea-Bissau and Cape Verde.

Mário de Andrade, who was an ever-present voice on several international platforms from the 1950s until independence and who made an important contribution to the universalization of the struggle against Portuguese colonialism, emphasizes the international dimension of Amílcar Cabral's actions and how the battles fought in the Portuguese colonies soon became part of the great epic of African emancipation as they spread beyond their boundaries, gained a universal resonance, and aroused the broadest and most diverse solidarity and hopes.

His background as a combatant, a committed intellectual, and the friend and companion of Cabral, means that Mário de Andrade is uniquely well placed to guide us through the origins and evolution of the political thought of the greatest figure in the history of Guinea-Bissau and Cape Verde.

This being so, *Amílcar Cabral—Essai de biographie politique* constitutes an extremely valuable resource for all those who wish to acquire or deepen their knowledge of the thought and praxis of the founder of the Cape Verde and Guinea-Bissau as independent countries, in the national and international context in which they developed.

The Engineer
of the Revolution

A teenage Amilcar Cabral wrote an epic poem about a young man
named "Fidemar," or "son of the sea." Trapped in poverty on the des-
olate island where he was born, Fidemar dreams of leaving his homeland to one day return as its salvation. Fidemar, the son of the sea, was
clearly an autobiographical figure for the young Cabral. As he was
writing the tale of escape and salvation, the Cabo Verde islands where
Cabral was raised were in the midst of one of the twentieth century's
most devastating famines. In the 1940s, roughly fifty thousand Cape
Verdeans—in a population of no more than three hundred thousand—died of hunger in a drought grossly exacerbated by Portuguese
colonial policy. For comparison, were a similar famine to take place
in the United States today, the equivalent death toll would be eighty
million, with over thirty million dying in the first year alone. Between
1920 and 1970, more Cape Verdeans died of hunger than lived on the
islands. This was the reality of Cabo Verde, and the reality of Fidemar
who fled in search of skills and experiences to transform the political
and economic conditions of a homeland in ruin. Tragically, as Cabral
writes it, Fidemar attempts to set out at sea and dies at just sixteen
years old. A few years after writing the story, Cabral would leave the
Cabo Verde islands and, like Fidemar, die before he would ever return
again. Unlike that son of the sea, Cabral would, over the course of his
short life, go on to be a protagonist of Africa's liberation from the last
vestiges of European colonial domination.

The revolutionary maxims of Amilcar Cabral (1924–73) are familiar to many: "tell no lies . . . claim no easy victories," "the people are

not fighting for ideas," "national liberation is necessarily an act of culture," "unity and struggle," and so on. However, fewer know the context from which his still-relevant ideas emerge. The basics of his short revolutionary life have been the subject of great adoration and general study by intellectuals and organizers in socialist, anticolonial, and Pan-African movements. Internationally and over the course of his short life, Cabral was increasingly recognized as a revolutionary leader par excellence in the tradition of Mao Zedong, Ho Chi Minh, and Fidel Castro. His assassination catapulted him to revolutionary martyrdom alongside the likes of Malcolm X, Dr. Martin Luther King, and Che Guevara. He was an inspiration to Pan-African revolutionary icons of the late 1970s and early 1980s such as Angela Davis, Amiri Baraka, and Thomas Sankara. Cabral continues to inspire thousands to this day, even being recognized by the bourgeois *BBC World Histories Magazine* as the "second greatest leader" in world history. But why? What was Amilcar Cabral's contribution to humanity and revolution that his name and image became so iconic and in the company of such world-historical figures?

In the context of the armed struggle against Portuguese colonialism in Africa from 1963–74, Cabral's African Party for the Independence of Guinea and Cabo Verde (PAIGC) was without question the most diplomatically, politically, and militarily successful liberation movement. Unlike its sister organizations in the Conference of Nationalist Organizations in the Portuguese Colonies (CONCP) such as the People's Movement for the Liberation of Angola (MPLA) and the Liberation Front of Mozambique (FRELIMO), the PAIGC was able to win an outright military victory against the Portuguese army. However, his leadership of the PAIGC—which was secretly founded by Cabral and five others in 1956—was not limited to Guinea and Cabo Verde, but was an integral part of the wider movement against Portuguese colonialism in Angola and Mozambique, and stood at the forefront of the worldwide socialist and anti-imperialist movement. Over the course of his brief political life, Cabral made a lasting impact on liberation struggles worldwide—leaving behind a legacy that revolutionaries are obligated to study and reflect upon as we build our own movements today.

Forty-four years after its initial publication in French, *Amílcar Cabral—Essai de biographie politique* by Mário Pinto de Andrade (a leading intellectual of the MPLA) remains without a doubt the preeminent synthesis and evaluation of the political thought and brilliance of the PAIGC secretary-general. But Andrade's "political biography" is not a cradle-to-grave accounting of every detail in Cabral's life, and he admits that there remains much to be uncovered by future historians.

Cabral did not write any manuscripts for publication aside from his master's thesis in agronomy on soil erosion, a time where he was reading Lenin's "On the Agrarian Question" as part of his political and academic study. His published writings consist of internal party documents, such as his 1965 and 1969 communiqués and lectures to party cadre; documents issued from the Party itself; and interviews and speeches given at international political bodies such as the UN or gatherings of revolutionaries from across the world. Cabral wrote to and for the Party. His unpublished writings, of which there are numerous—although many have surely been lost to history—consist of titles like "On Our Struggle Against the Helicopters," a handwritten forty-page memo on the military arena following Portugal's strategic shift to aerial bombardment of the Guinean rebels. His punchy quotations and timeless slogans served to correct or explain party behaviors, and to win international support for the Party's revolutionary cause: national liberation.

However, in *Amílcar Cabral—Essai de biographie politique*, Andrade offers us intimate insight into the political development of the revolutionary leader. The inaccessibility of this text to English-speaking and North American audiences until this point has left a major gap in the collective understanding of his life, particularly for an audience central to carrying on Cabral's commitment to building a socialist future and defeating imperialism: revolutionaries living in the center of global capitalism. It is through this endeavor of translation, that we seek to make Cabral's crucial intellectual and political interventions available to all interested in the development of Marxist theory and organizing in the Third World.

A Party Leader

In discussing what made Cabral a singularly important African revolutionary of his time, Andrade is consistent in emphasizing what has consistently been decentered: his leadership of a revolutionary socialist party. "The Party" formed by Cabral was "the most important instrument of liberation for his people," writes Andrade, who was the cofounder of the MPLA. On this point it is worth quoting Andrade at length, in his articulation of what made Cabral such a singular figure:

> The name of Amílcar Cabral is spontaneously associated with two great figures who marked the course of events in Africa in the 1960s with the imprint of their personalities: Patrice Lumumba, the martyr of the Congo, and Kwame Nkrumah, the [Ghanaian] visionary of Pan-African unity. These two great leaders shared Cabral's ardent passion for the cause of the liberation of colonized peoples. It is worth noting, however, that *Cabral's revolutionary heritage is distinguished from that of his illustrious contemporaries by a consistent contribution that took concrete form through the creation of a structured political party, the PAIGC* [emphasis added].

As Andrade points out, Cabral himself understood that in the balance sheet of strengths and weaknesses, it was the "party organization that dominates all other strengths" in the course of the liberation movement. Andrade's recognition that Cabral's greatest achievement was *the formation and leadership of the PAIGC* is one that is overlooked by most academics and not fully understood even by many organizers who profess to be followers of Cabral. That Andrade's own organization in his native Angola, the MPLA—which was notably not formed as a party but a "liberation movement"—was plagued by numerous internal struggles, splits, and failed alliances through its revolutionary history is no small consideration in understanding his admiration of the PAIGC. It is not just Cabral's individual brilliance which distinguishes him from revolutionary heroes such as Lumumba and Nkrumah, it is the collective weapon he was instrumental in forging: the Party. It was "through the creation of the Party" which, in Andrade's words and Cabral's practice, made it possible to "accomplish what in the eyes of the masses seemed to be impossible." It was "the Party" which became:

> [The] instrument capable of leading the masses to understand the nature of their own exploitation, then of mobiliz-

ing them, giving them a framework, a political consciousness so that they would support the war, of transforming
them into militants, and of founding the nation. A party,
the PAIGC, guided by a revolutionary theory.

Historicizing the Struggle

Parts I and II of *Amílcar Cabral: A Political Life in Motion* highlight
the colonial context in which Cabral grew up, the conditions which
made resistance to imperial domination an inevitability and shaped
the eventual contours which national liberation would take. Andrade
explains the sociopolitical climate in which the founding core of the
party garnered overt political experience in the colonial metropolis of
Lisbon through their initial attempts of clandestine study and struggle. The youth who Andrade termed the "Cabral generation"—future
leaders of the liberation movements in Portuguese Africa—literally
graduated at a time of great global tumult, as the Third World from
China to Cuba, Hanoi to Algiers, all began to awaken and rise up
against colonial and imperial dominance. Andrade regularly refers to
the initial "dogmatism" which plagued the attempts at organizing led
by Cabral and others—attempts to blindly replicate past revolutionary experiences without a careful consideration of their own concrete
conditions. Parts III and IV go into a historical and theoretical analysis of the national liberation struggle led by the PAIGC, its successes
building off of the accumulated experiences of past revolutionary
movements.

In this regard, the great victories of Cabral's lifetime were all
victories of the Party, as were his failures. Regarding the latter, the
1959 massacre of several dozen striking dock workers in Pidjiguiti,
Guinea, organized by the PAIGC, represents the last catastrophic
failure of Cabral's leadership until his January 1973 assassination at
the hands of colonial agents, counterrevolutionaries, and national
chauvinists still in the ranks of the Party. Cabral's inability to fully
protect himself and purge the Party of corrosive elements would
prove to be a decisive blow to the unity of the PAIGC which would
eventually split in 1980–81.

Nevertheless, Cabral's decade-plus leadership of the PAIGC was
filled with remarkable achievements for the Party-led national liberation movement. The failed labor action in Pidjiguiti laid bare the

impossibility and danger of acts of nonviolent civil disobedience and aboveground political action in the colonial context, and so the PAIGC spent over three years preparing for guerrilla warfare against the Portuguese. Party cadre organized underground in urban centers and were deployed to the countryside to organize the peasantry, a diverse social stratum which in Guinea Cabral had gotten to know better than any who had come before him, owing to his conducting of the country's first agricultural census while still an employee of the colonial state. It was because of this preparation that just six months after the PAIGC launched the armed struggle in Guinea, the Party seized nearly 15 percent of Guinean territory back from Portuguese colonial domination.

A year later, the PAIGC held its first party congress in Cassacá. Under Cabral's leadership, it was reorganized through purges of undisciplined and chauvinist—both male and tribal—party elements, as well as through a commitment towards building unity with the peasant masses in liberated zones where the Party established village assemblies, medical clinics, people's stores, people's tribunals, and village schools—none of which existed under Portuguese rule. Four years later, in 1968, the PAIGC had liberated roughly two-thirds of Guinean territory, creating a people's democracy where colonial dictatorship had existed prior. Following a fact-finding mission by the UN Special Mission in April 1972, the General Assembly decided on November 14 of that year to declare the PAIGC the "sole, genuine, and legitimate representative of Guinea and Cabo Verde." This was without ever having launched an armed struggle in Cape Verde, despite aborted attempts to do so.

Cabral would be assassinated in January of 1973, in the midst of setting up the independent state of Guinea amidst continued Portuguese occupation. Nevertheless, the PAIGC leadership would launch an aggressive military campaign named Operation Amílcar Cabral against remaining Portuguese military garrisons throughout the country, winning a decisive military victory by September 1973. The colonial fascist Estado Novo of Portugal would be overthrown a few months later on April 25, 1974, not coincidentally by junior military officers who had served and been routed by the PAIGC's Revolutionary Armed Forces of the People (FARP) trained by Cabral.

Developing Marxist Theory to Mobilize against Colonialism

But just as Cabral's political accomplishments were inextricably linked to his leadership of the Party, so too were the highlights of his intellectual legacy. Cabral's numerous contributions and interventions in the science of Marxism were not the thoughts of an intellectual divorced from struggle. He wrote to better his party and to offer his summations and assessments of the challenges of national liberation, all while summarizing and assessing the histories of liberation movements past. Like Lenin—who Andrade references in this political biography—Cabral engaged with revolutionary theory to sharpen revolutionary practice and vice versa, and this is exemplified in what is arguably his most famous speech, "Presuppositions and Objectives of National Liberation in Relation to Social Structure," now better known as "The Weapon of Theory." In it, Cabral tackled questions of ideology, class struggle, imperialism, history, and national liberation with stunning clarity to ultimately deliver his theory of "class suicide." This theory is one which has been deeply misunderstood, not only in its meaning, but in its *purpose*.

Cabral was primarily preoccupied with the question of the revolutionary petite bourgeoisie, a class which was an *over-determining* factor, not only in the Guinean revolution, but in African decolonization. This was not an abstract concern, but a direct response to the fact that the leadership of the PAIGC was not only disproportionately petite bourgeois in origin, but Cape Verdean in nationality leading a revolution in Guinea. This was a long-time concern in the socialist movement, dating back to Marx and Engels' 1879 letters to the German Social-Democratic Party leaders and 1850 address to the Communist League. Class suicide was not just a prognosis regarding the path which must be taken by the revolutionary petite bourgeoisie, but a diagnosis of the realities of decolonization, nation-building, and global political economy during the Cold War. As a class in the colonized world, the petite bourgeoisie does not have the capacity to control the mode of production—a factor which Cabral sees as the true motive force of history in his own intervention and contribution to Marx's analysis. That capacity lay only with two social groups: the global ruling class of imperialist capital and the oppressed native working class.

To commit to the historic mission entrusted upon it by the oppressed masses, the revolutionary petite bourgeoisie would have to commit "suicide," going against its own material interests and aspirations to become a comprador bourgeoisie, and forming and subjecting itself to the collective will of the native workers and peasants. This was Cabral's first major theoretical contribution to the intellectual tradition of revolutionary Marxism, made possible by a deep study of both general and specific conditions across Africa. And in the tradition of Marx and Lenin, it was done to sharpen the Party and further revolution. In this spirit, "The Weapon of Theory," delivered at the Tricontinental Conference in Havana in 1966, so impressed the Communist Party of Cuba that it earned Cabral a private audience with Fidel Castro and bolstered the bilateral relations between Cuba and the PAIGC, marking a concrete positive development in the liberation struggle led by the Party.

The political successes of Cabral's diplomatic travels, as in Havana, served as the foundation for his continued speechmaking and gave a glimpse into the Party's internal study and debate. In 1970 and 1972, Cabral traveled to the United States where he gave two of his most well-known speeches: "National Liberation and Culture," delivered at Syracuse University—in honor of Mozambican revolutionary Eduardo Mondlane—and "Identity and Dignity in the National liberation Struggle," delivered at Lincoln University—the alma mater of Kwame Nkrumah. It was in the United States where Cabral articulated his famous theorizations on culture and made such statements as "culture is simultaneously the fruit of a people's history and a determinant of history" and "national liberation is necessarily an act of culture;" and also where he articulated the theories of "re-Africanization" and the "return to the source." Cabral never wrote without having party concerns at the forefront of his mind. So why was culture a concern? Why then would Cabral spend so much time thinking about the problem of the "return to the source" or re-Africanization?

Cultural resistance was the backbone and "primary phase of the liberation movement," and it was waged most fiercely by the peasant masses of Guinea, or the 99 percent of the population who had the least contact with European culture or colonists. But considering what cultural resistance would look like, again, we return to the revolutionary petite bourgeoisie's over-determined role in the national liberation struggle and in the PAIGC. This was part of the national question within Guinea and Cabo Verde for there was a disproportionate amount of petit bourgeois Cape Verdeans in the leadership of the Party who, like Cabral, were children of, or they themselves "civil servants, members of the liberal professions, hired commercial employees, small agricultural owners. The fate of the revolution—as explained in "The Weapon of Theory"—relied on this class' identification with, not just the class interests of the working class and peasant masses, but their culture. And so, Cabral emphasized a re-Africanization, a "return to the source," a cultural turn that centered itself on a reclaimed sovereignty and looking to building a new future for the continent after decolonization.

The class component of culture was central as Cabral envisioned a counterrevolutionary alliance that could be built between the "senior civil servant or the assimilated intellectual" and the "traditional or religious leaders" of the countryside who represented the elite stratum of rural class society, despite the fact that the latter "experienced no significant foreign influence." The revolutionary alliance and subsequent merger of class and cultural interests had to be with the revolutionary petite bourgeoisie and the "mass of workers in the countryside and towns." This point was vital for the audience that Cabral delivered this address to: Black Americans. No doubt drawing from his Party's own experiences—particularly at its first congress at Cassacá where reactionary tribal and patriarchal elements were purged from the Party—and an international analysis of other liberation struggles, Cabral warned:

> The return to the source cannot in itself be an act of struggle against foreign domination, colonialist or racist. And it no longer necessarily means a return to traditions. It is a denial by the petite bourgeoisie of the pretended supremacy of the culture of the dominant power over that of the dominated people.

The return to the source, argues Cabral, was not an individual choice but "expressed in groups or movements, [where] the contradiction is transformed into struggle, secret or overt, and is a prelude to the pre-independence movement or of the struggle for liberation from the foreign yoke." This analysis was one deeply connected to the specific dilemmas of a party and liberation movement in an underdeveloped and primarily rural society where organized struggle and leadership was shaped by a tiny minority of civil servants, professionals, and intellectuals.

Cabral's Thought across the World and through History

Despite the specificity of the context he responded to, Cabral would go on to become revered by leading Black liberation organizers in the US, namely by Owusu Sadaukai and Amiri Baraka who were in attendance at Lincoln University and leaders of the African Liberation Support Committee. While it is impossible to transport the conditions of Cabral to the context of North America, the foundations of his thought came from a deep study of his own people and the applicable experiences of other liberation movements. The practical synthesis of this study was expressed by what Andrade called that "most important instrument of liberation": the Party.

Contextually, Andrade argues, the "Third World revolutionary experiences . . . of Vietnam most closely resembles" the case of Guinea. This "naturally meant that the theory and practice of the Việt Minh constituted the principal source of inspiration for Guinea-Bissau's revolutionary project." For this reason, Andrade dedicates an entire chapter to showing the revolutionary similarities and departures of theory and praxis between Cabral and the PAIGC and Nguyen Vo Giáp and the National Liberation Front (NLF). In Cabral's analysis, questions of the united front, the workers party, and the revolutionary army—all constants in the revolutionary Marxist tradition—were of the utmost importance. Andrade goes back to Engels and Marx to understand and situate Cabral in world history, including the secretary-general's "corrective to the famous proposition of *Communist Manifesto*," which Engels himself had begun to consider as early as 1888, that class struggle was the "motive force of history" only in a particular phase of history—that of class society. Refusing to place the Africans, Asians, and indigenous Americans who did not live in class societies "outside of history," Cabral "stretched Marxism," not to disagree with Marx and Engels, but to push their thought further, and named the "level of productive forces" as the "true and permanent motive force of history." The primary contradiction facing revolutionary socialists in the period of national liberation was not the struggle between classes domestically, but the struggle to regain control over the productive forces from an outside usurper—imperialism. Once achieved, these revolutionaries would be faced with the dual task of raising the productive forces and waging the class struggle against enemies, domestic and abroad, who seek to establish a neocolonial relationship. Unfortunately, Cabral never lived to face this task. But in laying out the presuppositions of national liberation in the African colonial context, Cabral showed himself to be a truly innovative contributor to Marxism not only in theory, but in the revolutionary praxis of the instrument he created: the PAIGC. Africans, whether living in communal, feudal, or class society, had a leading role to play in the struggle to claim their history and defeat imperialism.

The theoretical innovations and organizational clarity of Cabral were, according to Andrade, "illuminated by a conceptual device: *historical materialism.*" Historical materialism, that keystone of the Marxist tradition, is what "guided him in understanding the conditions of struggle and other cultural contributions," and was instrumental in his study and analysis of the Guinean countryside. Cabral's *Palavras de ordem gerais* (*General Watchwords*) and *Palestras no seminário de quadros* (*Lectures at Cadre Seminars*), both of which are regularly cited in this text, the latter of which is soon to be translated and published by 1804 Books, highlight the PAIGC leader's concrete application of historical materialism in his party work. This is what Andrade calls Cabral's "concrete analysis of the concrete situation." Cabral's brilliant analysis, captured here, that it was because of Portugal's own underdevelopment—which rendered it unable to practice neocolonialism like its British and French counterparts—why the national liberation struggle was dragged on for so long is one such example. Part IV highlights this specific colonial and also that national liberation was not an abstract phenomenon, but the liberation of the "productive forces" from imperialist domination. In this sense and others, Andrade unequivocally places Cabral in the lineage of Marx, Engels and Lenin, the torchbearers of the struggle against capitalism and imperialism—the struggle for socialism and national liberation. It is a torch which Cabral carried masterfully in his less than fifty years of physical existence, a mission for revolutionaries in the twenty-first century to complete in the face of impending climate and nuclear apocalypse.

It is especially fitting that 1804 Books publishes this historic text by Mário de Andrade in what we are calling The Year of Lenin and Cabral, a year commemorating the centennial of the former's death and the latter's birth. Few figures have made as significant a contribution as these two, separated by time and space, in the fight against capitalism and imperialism, and for socialism, national liberation, and revolutionary democracy. We hope that this text will be a tool so people can better contextualize the life of Cabral who, unlike Lenin, does not have thirty-five printed volumes of his work available to readers. Today it is urgent to read all of Cabral and study the context in which he lived and struggled, not just memorize his maxims. Cabral, the historical materialist. Cabral, the African. Cabral, the Party leader. Cabral, the revolutionary. Even Cabral, the agronomist. Andrade throughout this work often refers to Cabral as *O Engenhero*, or The Engineer, in reference to his educational and professional background. Cabral too was an engineer of revolution, the PAIGC being the engine he designed with liberation as its motive.

— *Desmond Fonseca*

CHRONOLOGY OF MAIN EVENTS (1954–1975)
The Struggle of the PAIGC

1954 Attempt to create a sports club, the Sports and Recreation Association, in Bissau.

November 1: proclamation of the insurrection of the Algerian people.

1955 Foundation of MING (Movement for the National Independence of Guinea).

Bandung Conference Meeting.

1956 September 19: creation of PAIGC in Bissau.

December: creation of the MPLA in Luanda.

1957 March 6: Independence of Ghana.

November: Consultation and Study Meeting for the Development of the Struggle Against Portuguese Colonialism, in which leaders from Angola, Mozambique, Guinea and the Islands of Cape Verde, and São Tomé participate.

Foundation of MAC (Anti-Colonial Movement).

December: First Conference of Afro-Asian Peoples, in Cairo.

1958   October 2: Proclamation of the Republic of Guinea.

December: Extended PAIGC meeting, where priority field mobilization is decided.

1960   January: Second session of the Conference of African Peoples, in Tunis.

Constitution of FRAIN (African Revolutionary Front for the National Independence of the Portuguese colonies).

October 4: Proclamation of Senegalese independence.

December 1: Appearance of the PAIGC information organ, *Libertação*.

1961   February 4: Triggering of armed struggle in Angola, under the direction of the MPLA.

April 18: Creation of the Conference of Nationalist Organizations of the Portuguese Colonies (CONCP) in Casablanca.

July 12–14: Conference of nationalist organizations from Guinea and the Cape Verde Islands, in Dakar.

August 3: Proclamation of direct action by PAIGC.

1962   January 15–30: Review of the program and statutes of the PAIGC, approved at a meeting of leading cadres.

June 25: Constitutive Congress of FRELIMO (Liberation Front of Mozambique).

July 6: Algerian independence.

1963   January 23: Attack on Tite's barracks by a commando unit. The beginning of the armed struggle in southern Guinea-Bissau.

May 25: Creation of the OAU (Organization of African Unity).

July: Opening of the northern front.

July 7–22: Staff meeting with the aim of studying the development of the struggle on the Cape Verde islands.

1964   January/March: Battle of Como.

February 13–17: First PAIGC Congress in Cassacá, in a liberated region in southern Guinea-Bissau.

September 25: Proclamation by FRELIMO of general armed insurrection in Mozambique.

November: Constitution of the first regular army units. Opening of the eastern front.

December: Publication of the first school book.

1965   March: Inauguration in Conakry of a boarding school for the children of the guerrillas.

August: Visit of the first OAU military mission to the liberated regions of Guinea-Bissau.

October 3–6: Second CONCP Conference in Dar-es-Salam.

1966   January 3: Creation of the Organization of Solidarity of the Peoples of Asia, Africa, and Latin America (OSPAAAL), in Havana.

September 19: Promulgation of the military justice law.

December: Reorganization of the People's Revolutionary Armed Forces (FARP).

1967   July 16: Inauguration of the radio station Rádio Libertação.

October: First delivery of weapons to the *tabanca* populations in the Quitáfine region (southern front).

1968   February 19: Attack on Bissalanca airport (10 km from Bissau) by a People's Army commando unit.

1969   February 3: Assassination of Eduardo Mondlane, president of FRELIMO.

February 5: Capture of the fortified camp of Madina do Boé, completing the liberation of the Boé region.

1970   June: International solidarity conference with the people of the Portuguese colonies, in Rome.

July 1: Pope Paul VI receives Amílcar Cabral, Agostinho Neto, and Marcelino dos Santos in an audience.

November 22: Portuguese aggression against Guinea-Conakry.

1971   August: Meeting of the Superior Council of Struggle, which adopts the decision to proclaim the new Independent State of Guinea-Bissau.

1972   April: Sending a UN mission to the liberated territories.

1973   January 20: Assassination of Amílcar Cabral in Conakry, by agents of the Portuguese colonialists.

February 7–9: The Party's national leadership launches the slogan of widespread action on all fronts.

May 25: Operation "Amílcar Cabral," which culminates in the capture of the Guiledje camp. Increased anti-aircraft defense.

July 18–22: Second PAIGC Congress in the liberated regions of the east. Aristides Pereira is unanimously elected General Secretary.

September 23–24: Meeting of the first National Popular Assembly of Guinea-Bissau in Madina Boé.

September 24, 8:55 GMT: Proclamation of the State of Guinea-Bissau. Luís Cabral is elected president of the State Council.

1974   January/February: Intensification of direct action in urban centers, while international recognition of the new state continues to be registered.

April 25: Overthrow of fascism in Portugal, whose internal situation had deteriorated with the colonial wars.

May 6–17: Meeting of Aristides Pereira, Secretary-General of PAIGC, with Mário Soares, Portuguese Minister of Foreign Affairs, in Dakar.

May 25–31: Start of talks in London between Pedro Pires, deputy commissioner of the armed forces, and Mário Soares.

June 13–14: First negotiations in Algiers.

August 9: (Secret) negotiations resume in Algiers.

August 23: Last phase of the Algiers negotiations.

August 26: Signing of the Algiers agreement by which Lisbon recognizes the independence of Guinea-Bissau and reaffirms the right of the people of the Cape Verde islands to self-determination and independence.

September 10: De jure recognition of Guinea-Bissau's independence from Portugal.

September 24: The first anniversary of Guinea-Bissau's independence is celebrated in Boé.

December 19: Signing of the agreement between the Portuguese government and the African Independence Party of Guinea and Cape Verde that recognizes the people of Cape Verde the right to self-determination and independence.

1975   January: Installation of the Transitional Government in Cape Verde.

June 30: Elections to the Constituent Assembly

July 5: Proclamation of the Independence of Cape Verde.

Preface

Today it is generally recognized that the victory of the armed struggles for national liberation carried out in Angola, Guinea-Bissau, and Mozambique constitutes one of the greatest events in contemporary history. Several factors make this a fair assessment: this victory allowed the African peoples of the former Portuguese colonies to take their own destinies in hand, it contributed decisively to the triggering of the democratic process in Portugal, and it shook the foundations of the imperialist strategy in Southern Africa.

The path to victory was, however, not an easy one. The struggle of these peoples took place at a time when the scope of confrontations in the Third World was evaluated in terms of the Western power at stake. However, in Guinea-Bissau, a country of modest geographical dimensions, African guerrilla fighters, mostly from the peasantry, defeated a classical European army supported by its North Atlantic Treaty Organization (NATO) allies. At the same time, they implemented the new social project that prefigured the current revolutionary national democracy in the regions that they had liberated.

The militant determination of a man and the strength of his thought lies at the root of this undertaking: the life and work of Amílcar Cabral. His life unfolded in a harmonious dialectical unity, containing and illuminating the meaning of his work.

As an artisan of the revolutionary consciousness of the masses, Cabral dedicated his creative energy, intellectual capacities, and political experience to the task that he had set himself: guiding the people of Guinea-Bissau and Cape Verde in the fight for the right to own their own history. This meant that he would become at once the unifier of men, as well as the political, theoretical, and practical leader of the armed struggle for national liberation. Endowed with an exceptional sense of organization, he managed to make the PAIGC into a body that vibrated to the tune of the interests of the popular masses. As President of the State Council of the Republic of Guinea-Bissau Luís Cabral, Amílcar's brother, is in the habit of saying *"the work of the founder of the nation lives on beyond his death."*

The name of Amílcar Cabral is spontaneously associated with two great figures who marked the course of events in Africa in the 1960s with the imprint of their personalities: Patrice Lumumba, the martyr of the Congo, and Kwame Nkrumah, the visionary of Pan-African unity. These two great leaders shared Cabral's ardent passion for the cause of the liberation of colonized peoples. It is worth noting, however, that Cabral's revolutionary heritage is distinguished from that of his illustrious contemporaries by a consistent contribution that took concrete form through the creation of a structured political party, the PAIGC. At the head of that party, a collective leadership was able to successfully drive the armed struggle for national liberation which accelerated the nation-forming process and led to the emergence of the states of Guinea-Bissau and Cape Verde.

According to Cabral, the African Party for the Independence of Guinea and Cape Verde (PAIGC) aimed to fulfill the historic duty of understanding the country's reality in order to transform it in the direction of progress and justice. Putting to one side the modesty of this statement, the depth of Cabral's actions and their lessons for all those who fight imperialist domination are clear to see.

As a privileged social actor in the history made both by the masses and in the light of his ideas, Cabral always carried out in deeds what he had proposed in words. This made it easy for us to go through the great stages that marked out his life to reveal the connections between political praxis and reflections on its meaning.

Starting from an analysis of the writings of both his youth and later texts to key moments during his leadership, this work aims to map Cabral's political and intellectual journey. We entrust to future historians the task of delving deeper into all the aspects raised here, which make up the originality of Cabral's contributions to such diverse fields as agronomy, political sociology, and military strategy.

Our biographical outline will limit itself to capturing the démarche of Cabral's personality, which, having modeled the historical development of his people, now provides progressive militants in the Third World with a theoretical weapon for the liquidation of oppressive regimes.

— *M. d. A.*

I wish to express my deep gratitude to Presidents Aristides Pereira and Luís Cabral for their constant encouragement, political trust, and intellectual contributions that allowed me to write this book.

Part I.
The Emergence of the Unifier

The interest of biography seems to stand directly opposed to a universal purpose; it, however, has indeed the historical world as a background with which the individual is involved.

— G. W. F. HEGEL

ONE

Roots

In order to understand Cabral's life and work in all their dimensions, we must first restore the general context of the times in which his personality was formed.

The social origins of his ancestry are specific to the history of the decline of classical colonialism in the islands of Cape Verde and Guinea-Bissau.

The family of his father, Juvenal Lopes Cabral, represents a typical product of the contradictions of the slave society that was established over more than four centuries on those islands. When Juvenal was born, it was also the family of a rich landowner: his grandfather. Nonetheless, Juvenal would later refer himself strictly as "an obscure elementary school teacher without a degree." Cape Verdean colonial society was plagued by chronic crises that for many years had forced islanders to emigrate. Thus, Juvenal went to Guinea in search of work. There he met his future wife, Amílcar's mother, Iva Pinhel Évora, originally from Praia, on the island of Santiago.* Amílcar's father played a leading role in forming his character.

Having benefited in his childhood from social privileges usually motivated by what is conventionally called "good fortune," Juvenal Cabral's studies had left him with a pronounced taste for literature. This led him to publish a work[1] which, among its autobiographical passages, nuanced by erudite notes and evocative reflections, addresses the problems of his time and his milieu.

---

* The capital of Cabo Verde

1

For us, *Memórias e reflexões* is more than mere testimony, it is a primary source that enables us to locate Amílcar Cabral's social origins:

> . . . it is certainly not a valuable book, the author writes in the foreword, worthy of taking its place among the good books of its kind. The author, an African by race, a son of Cape Verde, without the literary resources that would enable him to triumph, beaten down by the waves of atrocious misfortune, regards himself as a simple "recruit" among the writers who ostentatiously line up in the wings alongside the professionals.

This modest confession is belied by the author's elaborate style, full of lyrical flights, in accordance with the canons of Portuguese literature of his time. Juvenal appeared at a time when, in the eyes of the West, Africa—and the Cape Verde archipelago—had never had a history, past, or culture of its own. Only one path was available to the young Juvenal: unrestricted cultural integration into the values of the "metropolis." He described his ancestry in the following term:

> Capricorn was walking serenely through the area of its influence in the vastness of the sky when I came into this world. It was six in the morning on January 2, 1889.

> To give due credit to astrology, I owe the ups and downs of my life to this mischievous and playful star sign, even more than to the rough housing I've suffered at the hands of wicked villains.

> *Homo homini lupus . . .*

> My mother, Rufina Lopes Cabral, belonged to a family of farmers from Ribeira do Engenho, on the island of São Tiago, where they had their own assets that, later, as was the case for so many, disappeared in the maelstrom. She then moved to the island of São Nicolau where she met my father, António Lopes da Costa, who was finishing his course at the seminary.

My father was the son of Pedro Lopes da Costa, a farmer and merchant, and one of the few Cape Verdeans who, in those distant times, paid serious attention to their children's education.

In the Lopes da Costa family, there were distinguished priests, teachers, and employees who did their best to serve and honor the Fatherland.

Fate did not want me to meet the author of my days by death in a disaster, possibly caused by criminals, which would substantiate an insistent and persistent rumor when I was just ten months old. Baptized sometime after the tragedy in which my father was the sacrificial lamb in the precipitous gorge of Cutelo Branco, I was given the name that he himself had chosen, an admirer as he was of that brilliant Latin poet.[2]

My grandfather, Pedro Lopes da Costa, knowing that I was fatherless, did not leave me helpless. He delivered me to the care of Dona Simoa dos Reis Borges, my godmother, and Paula Lopes da Costa, my aunt, who, with another older sister, Dona Maria Nozoline dos Reis Borges, lived in Godim, together with their mother, Dona Adaiama Gomes dos Santos.[3]

At the age of nine, Juvenal was taken to Portugal to attend the primary school of São Tiago de Cassurrães, a "working village in Beira Alta" where he was the first and only black boy among forty white boys. He then entered the seminary in Viseu, being destined, according to the wishes of his adoptive family, for ecclesiastical life. According to his own testimony, he spent "the best days of his life" there.

Pedro Lopes da Costa, who died in 1900, bequeathed the sum of six hundred thousand *réis*[4] to his grandson. The burden of Juvenal's education was entirely borne by his godmother, Dona Simoa, especially since she and her sister inherited the assets of her brother, Manuel dos Reis Borges, a rich and generous man, a "great man of Cape Verde, an authentic potentate in Santa Catarina and surrounding areas [. . .] always dressed in a tailcoat and bowler hat." It is to those "ladies of high virtues" that Juvenal Cabral owed the "literary knowledge" that would later allow him to enter public life.

But, at the turn of the century, drought devastated the land and the populations of the islands, making it impossible for his tutors to send him the necessary funds to continue his studies. Juvenal returned to the archipelago without having finished the preparatory course and went on to attend another seminary—São Nicolau—in 1906. However, he abandoned his studies the following year and returned to Godim, in Santiago, one morning in July. He was then eighteen years old.

In April 1911, Juvenal Cabral decided to embark for Guinea-Bissau in search of work.

He started out as a public servant in Bolama, second provisional aspirant at the Higher Finance Department.[5] Later appointed second provisional trainee of the customs staff and posted in Bissau. He was dismissed from this position by order of the Government Supervisor on October 24, 1913.[6] At the end of that year, he became the first teacher at the Cacine elementary school, whose roll included a mere half-dozen students. On the subject of the monotonous and sometimes boring life of the area, he wrote:

> We—the administrator, the clerk, the telegraph operator, the head of the customs post, the teacher, the nurse, and a shopkeeper—accounted for the entirety of the census data on the population that, alongside a small family, lived in the five houses in the district headquarters![7]

Juvenal Cabral, "an obscure elementary school teacher without a degree," taught in other regions in Guinea-Bissau, and provided ethnographic information about them.

> . . . the town of Bafatá, headquarters of the Civil District of the same name, a commercial center of the first order stands like an amphitheater, smiling and prosperous, at the point where the small river Colufi joins its waters to those of the much larger Geba, whose winding banks bore witness to interesting historical events.[8]

Amílcar was born in Bafatá on September 12, 1924.[9] In 1931, Juvenal Cabral was in charge of the School Treasury of Bissau and respective bookkeeping. He recalled this in the pamphlet[10] in which he defended himself against an accusation that he owed money (in the amount of 7,450 *réis*) to his colleague, D. Maria Baptista da Câmara, "a distinguished professor of *fencing* who is not afraid to pierce the heart of honor with a deadly lunge!" The controversy surrounded a loan (later repaid) which had been motivated by the urgent need to send his sick family (wife and child), which was soon to grow in number, to Cape Verde. Having inherited the assets of his godmother, Dona Simoa dos Reis Borges—rural properties and real estate—Juvenal Cabral had to manage them. To this end, he returned to his native island of Santiago in November 1932, where he would remain until his retirement.[11] But he progressively lost the material benefits of his inheritance, as he found literature and the good life much more exciting than business. He was also extremely generous to the disadvantaged in the area.

Some extracts from correspondence exchanged with landowners in the 1940s attest to increasing financial difficulties.

The Cabral family experienced the Second World War at the same time as the catastrophes that befell the Cape Verdean people. In the political double game played by the Salazar government, Portugal's neutrality meant supplying the products of its colonies to both the Axis and the Allies. This resulted in a dizzying rise in the cost of living and scarce availability of staple foods. Two key factors shook the colonized society of the Archipelago: the repercussions of the war, on the one hand, and the direct consequences of drought leading to cyclical crises of hunger, on the other. In 1940, the crisis claimed the lives of 20,000 out of a total population of 180,000. In the following year, people recovered, only to fall victim to another crisis, this time lasting from 1942 to 1948 and leading to the deaths of 30,000 victims. Throughout the world conflagration and during the period following it, 50,000 people in the Archipelago died of hunger. In addition to these catastrophes, rationing was imposed by the local government.

War revealed the true face of Portuguese colonialism. Even though the Lisbon government presented Cape Verde as benefiting from a status comparable to the adjacent islands of the Azores and Madeira—and therefore not exactly a colony—military occupation by the expeditionary corps exposed this as mere propaganda. The physical presence of colonial troops, which engendered racism, violent clashes with the population, and manifestations of contempt from island society, reactivated regionalist feelings and led to constant provocations of Cape Verdeans' dignity. Information subtly conveyed by [the colonial] administration led the Portuguese soldiers to believe that they constituted a deterrent to the danger of a Nazi invasion. The troops were primarily billeted at Porto Grande (on the island of São Vicente), Praia, and Sal airports. The psychological impact of this foreign presence greatly disturbed the spirit of the Cape Verdean population.

Drought and famine brought other catastrophes: an *assistência* building in Praia that provided a refuge to people fleeing drought collapsed under the weight of the huge number of inhabitants, leading to hundreds dying under the ruins.* Forced emigration to plantations in São Tomé and Angola began, especially since the freedom to emigrate to North America had been restricted.

The Cape Verdean musical form known as the *morna*** recorded the details of this forced emigration.[12]

> *Quato ora di madrugada*
> *Djentes S. Vicente em pê*
> *Ta grita, tâ tchora*
> *Spêra largada di sês fidjo pâ S.*
> *Tomé. Grande rabolice na vóvó*
> *Por causa di nhô Mota Carmo*
> *Qu'ré trâ S. Vicente sê povo*
> *Djudado pâ sês catchôr . . .*
>
> *Wilson ê cais pâ carvon*
> *Pâ povo câ ficâ*

---

* The tragic collapse of the assistência building, which served as a welfare office and soup kitchen, happened on February 20, 1949.

** Morna is a national genre of Cape Verde characterized by the singing of blues normally over a piano, violin and a rhythmic guitar section. Many mornas are lamentations over the hardships of life and love on the islands. Amílcar Cabral wrote a poem, "Regresso," which was later performed as a morna by the world famous Cape Verdean singer, Cesaria Evora.

discontenti
Lá ês embarcâ sê coraçon . . .***

As we will see later, the spectacle of hunger constituted, without a shadow of a doubt, the primary foundation of the revolt in the intellectual and political trajectory of the young Amílcar.

Juvenal Cabral—not one to passively submit to fate—expressed his fearless opinion about hunger with courage and clarity, as "like a vulture stalking its prey, it tries to establish itself among the people." The hunger naturally caused a drop in agricultural production. In December 1940, he sent a memorandum to the governor of the colony, Major Amadeu Gomes de Figueiredo, in which he issued the following predictions:

> Cape Verde, despite the sovereign desires of its rulers to modify its living conditions, following the course set by its mysterious destiny, finds itself, from time to time, face to face with the terrifying vision of hunger. Every twenty years—the chronicles say—the people of Cape Verde are overwhelmed by the rigors of famine. The facts, in general, contribute to confirming tradition. In our century, two famines occurred within the time period predicted by the ancients: that of 1902 and that of 1922.
>
> [. . .] As we stand on the threshold of 1941, the desolate aspect of the coastal fields, like many others in the interior of the island, clearly announces the advent of a new and horrifying catastrophe. And the people tremble at the memory of the tradition that, once again, promises to be confirmed![13]

***   "At the break of dawn
the people of São Vicente got up
They scream and cry
waiting for their children to leave for São Tomé. There are major disturbances in the prison
Because of governor Mota Carmo
who wants to take its people from São Vicente
helped by their dogs . . .

Wilson's pier is destined for coal
But so that the people don't revolt
Then they (the colonialists) secretly embarked on the hearts of the people."

Literal translation from Cape Verde creole to Portuguese by Maria Dulce Almada. See: PAIGC Declaration before the UN Special Committee of June, 1962.

He would later write:

> . . . And the tradition was confirmed, eloquently, in the
> devastating famine of 1942!!

In December 1941, Juvenal Cabral wrote another memorial, an "obscure document" that was delivered to the then Minister of Colonies, Francisco Vieira Machado, who was on a visit to Santiago. In his capacity as "Cape Verdean by birth and race," he proposed to speak to the Minister "with frankness and simplicity, the characteristics of noble and sensitive hearts." And thus, he went on:

> . . . Cape Verde . . . now feels prey to extremely cruel appre-
> hensions, given the effects arising from this Hydra who,
> insensitive and implacable, has established himself among
> men, and bears the fateful name of Crisis.[14]

Although he knows that the "central government intends to destroy this infernal hydra that is hunger, always devastating and always cruel," he continues in these terms:

> Unfortunately, the evils that affect and atrophy the eco-
> nomic life of the Cape Verdean Archipelago are long-
> standing. So much so, that the prosperity of its commerce
> and agriculture, unable to create deep roots, have the
> ephemeral duration of a flower whipped by a gale.[15]

For this reason, Juvenal Cabral drew attention to the solution of a certain number of problems of transcendent importance "for the economic equilibrium of the Archipelago." What problems? It is worth mentioning them in full:

a) Water prospecting and collection. The lack of water
    for irrigation of crop fields is, in my opinion, one of
    Cape Verde's gravest problems.
b) Intensive afforestation, using *Jatropha* for the pasture
    fields and coconut trees for the streams that border
    the sea. The coconut tree grows rapidly on the coast

and its precious fruit can contribute to alleviating
people's difficulties, especially in times of famine.

c)   The protection of agriculture, starting with a review
and reorganization of building matrices. The taxes
recently levied on rural properties, in the condition
that they are in, constitute an inhumane scourge
afflicting the farmers of this island of São Tiago.

d)   Exemption from payment of rural property tax this
year, in which agricultural production is zero and
owners are devoid of resources.

e)   Creation of long-term agricultural credit, which
allows the development of rural properties.

f)   Protection for small employees who, in Cape Verde, live
in precarious and peripatetic circumstances. There are
employees who, after paying their monthly expenses,
cannot save ten *escudos* for treats for their children.[16]

Between emigration and the drought—or in Juvenal Cabral's expression, "the rigors of famine"—hunger spread and crushed the Cape
Verdean people.[17]

Such was the socioeconomic and historical context of the archipelago in which Amílcar Cabral's adolescence and emerging youth
unfolded.*

Hitherto, we have discussed the influence exerted by his father
in the intellectual formation and even in the guidance that led him
to choose to study agronomy. We must not overlook the role of that
Woman who was the *star* of his *rustic childhood*: his mother, Dona Iva
Pinhel Évora.[18] Once he had completed his elementary education in
the city of Praia, Amílcar continued his secondary studies in Mindelo,
in São Vicente, (at the Liceu Infante D. Henrique, later known as Gil
Eanes).[19] It was essentially during this period (from the mid-1930s
until the end of the Second World War) that, in Amílcar's eyes,
Dona Iva's personality assumed the importance of a mother entirely
dedicated to protecting him against the vicissitudes of fortune and
preparing him for life.

---

*   In one of his 1969 lectures to PAIGC cadre, Cabral explicitly mentions that the specter of hunger and famine
directly inspired his revolt against Portuguese colonialism. In that lecture, he notes that, in the last fifty years, more
people died of hunger in Cape Verde than currently lived on the islands.

Clinging to her sewing machine, Dona Iva "set traps against hunger," as the words of the René Depestre song go.[20] She was the embodiment of the recurring image of the humble seamstress that the poets from the tropical belt of extreme poverty know so well. Thus, Aimé Césaire wrote:

> . . . and my mother, whose legs pedal without rest for the sake of our hunger, that pedal day and night, I am even woken up at night by these indefatigable legs that pedal at night and the acrid bite in the soft flesh of the night of the Singer sewing machine that my mother pedals, pedals for our hunger day and night.[21]

Amílcar's mother was, however, obliged to accept a more remunerative job in a fish cannery. As a way of illustrating the economic reality of Cape Verde during the Second World War, Amílcar Cabral spoke about Dona Iva's case to young PAIGC fighters:

> . . . And to better understand the shamelessness of the Portuguese, I remember, for example, that when I was in high school, my mother went to Cape Verde, got a job in the fish canning factory, because sewing wouldn't earn enough. And do you know how much she earned per hour? Five pennies per hour, and, if there were a lot of fish, she could work eight hours a day and take home four pesos. But if there wasn't much fish (and she had to walk a long way to get to the factory), she would work for one hour and earn five *tostões*.[22]

A brilliant student, Amílcar combined his intelligence and dedication to work with an extreme sensitivity to the social environment around him. The fundamental traits of his personality are revealed in his first attempt at poetry and fiction, which express his search for himself and an affirmation of his regional character—his *caboverdianidade* (Cape Verdeanness).

Let us take a brief look at his writings from this period, which have more of a family feel than those of his father and express how he, a secondary school student, sees his first loves and situates himself in relation to the islands and the world.

Two incomplete notebooks of poetry, laboriously typed, shed light on the youthful loves of "Larbac," an anagram of "Cabral." The titles are significant in themselves: *In the Intervals of the Art of Minerva* that, according to Cabral himself are "the product of weak inspiration, the echo of the voice of a lyre, which, played in the intervals of study, tries to express part of the feelings of a youthful chest, belonging to a new generation. . . . "; *When Cupid Hits the Target . . .* , which contains only part of the poem "Daydreams," provides a chronological and spatial indication: 1940/43, Mindelo.

The first book (which originally had at least eighteen pages) opens with a preamble in the form of a letter addressed to his friend Coutinho[23] who, according to the context of the writing, exercised a degree of literary authority over Amílcar Cabral:

> . . . If today, in an almost unconscious act, I dare to place my unpretentious verses under the dark wings of criticism, I cannot help but record, at the top of the first page of my book, as in a literary landmark, the following words:

> To you, friend of good fortune and misfortune, only to you I owe this satisfaction to the courage you have always instilled in me, to the valiant support you have always given me in matters relating to my (vain?) literary career.

And in conclusion:

> I did as you asked. And, as this is the first time that I have ventured to face criticism, I exclaim:

> *Alea jacta est!*

A part of Amílcar's contribution to the "forgotten and small literature" of Cape Verde falls within the domain of lyricism. Influenced,

---

*   The die is cast

naturally, by his reading at school[24] (Casimiro de Abreu, Gonçalves Crespo, Guerra Junqueiro, and other Portuguese and Brazilian authors from literary selections), he expressed, in well-rhymed verses, his "time of love," as in the last stanzas of the "Sonnet MCMXLIII" dedicated to his muse Lamaria:

Vem tu, que foste o santo amor d'outrora
o meu amor mais louco neste mundo
e que és todo o esplendor do meu sacrário!

Vem embalar-me, ó deusa, vem,
aurora trazer-me o teu olhar divino e
jocundo, tirar-me este sofrer, o meu
calvário! . . .

It is still in the lyrical tone that Amílcar restores to us the atmosphere then prevailing in Mindelo and Praia—the obsessive presence of the sea!

É a única estrada
que acalenta o sonhar deste povo . . .
Para nós é a única estrada que promete evasão . . .

His prose writings, whether in the form of notes or fiction, seem to us more significant for his time and perhaps more enlightening for understanding his vision of the insular *universe*. Affirming the right of Cape Verdeans to write about Cape Verde, Amílcar explains himself in these terms: " . . . because it is right, naturally right, for a man to condemn or praise everything that concerns the earth, his Mother, the people, his brother, and, finally, he himself."[25]

For this reason, he points out and comments on *facts*. The first of these is a critical description around the "extraordinary movement"

---

* Come, you who were the sacred love of the past,
my craziest love in this world
and that you are all the splendor of my tabernacle!

Come and sway me, oh goddess, come,
dawn, bring me your divine and joyful gaze, take away this suffering, my calvary! . . .

** It is the only road
that soothes the dreams of these people...
For us it is the only road which promises escape...

on the Praia pier. It is, in effect, the indignant record of his impressions regarding the work of the sailors and dockers as they unloaded the goods from the *Bissau* anchored in the bay. His observations have social connotations.

> . . . It is curious to note the similarity between the case of this boat and another frequent case in Cape Verde: that of the replacement of employees with good service records by foolish new employees simply because the boss had not got along well with the old ones, or because it is convenient to employ the new ones in order to please the "godparents" . . .

He ends on an optimistic note:

> . . . There is a pause in the music of life, and the notes beat tirelessly against the pillars of the fountain, the times of this pause that will end tomorrow, at the break of dawn. . . .

The untitled story in which Amílcar, when portraying the life of a sixteen-year-old boy, projects himself, so to speak, onto this character, was probably written before 1943: Fidemar [son of the sea].

> *Mergulhador* had an enormous will to live.

> But [his will] to live a life unlike the one he led, a life he passionately aspired to, an aspiration that made him different from others—that made him a revolutionary.

> This sixteen-year-old boy was a revolutionary. He stood out in the environment in which he lived due to his way of being and his hatred for everything that was contrary to his aspiration for freedom and life for all.

In the Mindelo of his youth—a narrow space in which his first emancipatory ideas matured—Amílcar took pains to paint a portrait of a typical *crioulo*, a son of the people, a defender of the poor and the weak, a sea captain:

One day the sea will conquer the land . . .

A true visionary, imbued with generous ideas:

> . . . Sitting there in the dark rectangle formed by the old
> boards under the pier, he was able to calm the anger he felt
> at not being able to renew everything he saw around him, at
> not being able to gather his friends together and tell them:

> Brothers. The life we live is one of great poverty. We are
> men, just like the others and, like them, we have the right
> to happiness. Let us no longer suffer in silence. Let us rebel
> and put an end to the injustice of men. Let us show the rich
> that, without the work of our parents, without our effort,
> they would not live. . . .

The wonderful world he dreamed of—the one he aspired to—could
not be a reality without a struggle. Hence the decision to leave and
then return stronger. However, the departure on a Greek boat resulted
in tragedy:

> While a stain of blood on the sea testified to Fidemar's
> death, in Chica's hut a little boy was born . . . with no
> father. He would know little about his mother. He was
> another son of the sea, another revolutionary perhaps . . .

This tale represents, to a certain extent, the archetype of the *possible*
hero in Amílcar's youth. Step by step it brings together a denunciation
of social injustices, a panorama of the life of the boys of São Vicente,
and the emergence of a figure who brings men together. But the
tragedy in the island universe is integrated into the fabric of everyday
life: the gigantic effort of the populations to survive in the aridity
of their motherland, described as "slivers of land that maps barely
register." Hence his handling of fiction. By opting for a dénouement
featuring a failed escape, could it be that Cabral wanted to reveal the
impossibility of the solutions germinating in Fidemar's mind?

In a different style and addressing a less "revolutionary" theme, the
short story entitled "Marias" dates from September 9, 1943.

In the midst of the account of amorous adventures attributed to a fellow student, Amílcar expresses anti-conformist considerations:

> . . . It was a *morna*, this loving, slow, lulling, soft, and warm music, this rhythmic translation of the feelings of a people who suffer to live and live to suffer resignedly—a stupid resignation that the new generation will exterminate!

—the miserable life that destiny had mapped out for it . . .

Dated October 26, 1944, and initially untitled, the text entitled *"Hoje e amanhã"* [Today and Tomorrow] was later published in the *Boletim da Casa dos Estudantes do Império Mensagem*[26] (with the undoubtedly incorrect mention of the date of October 1945). Using the pseudonym "Arlindo António," Cabral begins the article with a brief "Letter to Afar," addressed to himself:

> . . . the World does not stop and, if it is true that your desires (of millions of men, as you say) still have a reason to exist, it is also true that, with each day that passes, man has greater awareness of his problems, and this fact alone is already moving forward. . . .

And this postscript:

> May your son (do you already have one?) be able to live tomorrow in the world you long for . . .

We can say, without a doubt, that here we see Amílcar's first philosophical reflection, an interrogation about the disturbing situation of a world set on fire by the Second World War and men's aspirations for a future of universal harmony. At the center of this reflection lies the idea of having a child, a bearer of hope for tomorrow, "one of the cells that will prepare material for the reconstruction of the world." As for the young people of his time, this idea of a son also finds its motivation in a certain morbid meditation on existential contingency. Thus, he writes, in his father's style:

> . . . I'm in my twenties and nothing guarantees that I'll
> be able to climb the upward slope of life, turn the hill, go
> straight down the slope of the other side—which is old
> age—and, after having lived, enter, crossing the line of
> nothingness that separates being from non-being, into the
> dark plain that is death.

Amílcar turned twenty when the Second World War entered its last
and most violent year. Never, in the course of history, had men achieved
such great destructive power. The corpses were counted in millions.

But the sinister cries of the international conflagration arrived
considerably deafened on the islands of Cape Verde, out of time, devastated by a scourge from other eras: hunger.

Despite this isolation, Amílcar was aware of the extent of the
hostilities and the nature of the conflict which he saw as a "sadly necessary event" in the class struggle—a notion that was still confused in
his mind but which was part of his considerations. A certain poetic
idealism predominated in his thoughts, the certainty of the tomor-
rows that people sang about, the inevitable *remodeling* of the world,
the new order emerging from the chaos[27] . . .

And the philosophical writing ends thus:

> Today, however, fighting reigns. The war of cannons and
> bombs, the war of ideas. . . . The struggle. Everywhere the
> struggle. Everywhere there is suffering and struggle.
>
> . . . In a future and next world that my child will be a part
> of, he or she may write: To Life. Everywhere life. Every-
> where there is happiness and life.[28]

Such were the ideas of young Amílcar. In the 1943–44 school year, he
completed his general secondary school course, obtaining a grade of 17
out of a possible 18. His reputation as a brilliant student would remain
etched in the collective memory of the islanders for a long time.[29]

Cabral returned to Praia. He worked as a trainee in the services of
the Imprensa Nacional [National Press],[30] where he endured bureau-
cracy and sometimes suffered humiliation from officials who allowed
themselves to correct his prose! . . . However, he continued to dedicate

himself to literature and dedicated one of his poems, published in a weekly newspaper in the Azores,[31] to João de Deus Lopes da Silva (brother of the writer Baltasar), commander of the sailing boat *Nossa Senhora dos Anjos*:

Tu vives—mãe adormecida—nua e esquecida,
seca,
batida pelos ventos,
ao som das músicas sem música das águas *que nos prendem* . . .
. . . .
Ilha:
colinas sem fim de terra vermelha
—terra bruta—
rochas escarpadas tapando os horizontes
mar aos quatro cantos prendendo as nossas ânsias!*

The theme of the powerless mother island, which feeds the dreams of those who will change the face of the archipelago, haunted Amílcar Cabral. Finally, in the autumn of 1945, after some degree of difficulty, he received a scholarship and departed for Lisbon. The choice of what he was to study at university had already been decided (undoubtedly with the agreement or complicity of his father): he would become an agricultural engineer.

---

* You live—sleeping mother—
naked and forgotten,
dry,
pummeled by the winds,
to the sound of the musicless songs of the waters that hold us . . .

Island:
endless hills of red earth
—raw land—
rugged rocks obscuring the horizons
sea at four corners, holding back our desires!

TWO

Cultural and Political Education

In the years immediately following the Second World War, Portugal, despite the fallacious "neutrality" of the Salazar government, did not find itself sheltered from the immense wave of progressive hopes that the Allies' victory over Nazism aroused throughout the world. Mass demonstrations in favor of democratic freedoms occurred one after the other, but soon the repressive apparatus forced the various movements underground. Political activists learned to fine-tune their weapons and test their courage in the harsh schools of prison and clandestine survival.

In this climate, Cabral became familiar with the Portuguese resistance to fascism. As soon as he entered the Instituto Superior de Agronomia [The Higher Institute of Agronomy] in the 1945–46 academic year, he joined in the demands of academic youth. One of his classmates, who later became his first wife, Dona Maria Helena Vilhena Rodrigues, declared:[32]

> I met Amílcar in the first year of the Agronomy course, in 1945. We started in the same year. Classes started in November, and I remember that Amílcar arrived much later, in December, from Cape Verde. That year a lot of people came—220 students, exactly 200 boys and 20 girls. We weren't in the same class, but I remember perfectly seeing him among the others; he was the only black person there, so he was very conspicuous . . . Amílcar did not take

the entrance exam. He did very well in the first General Mathematics exam, he got 12 or 13, one of the highest grades. People started talking about him. He was a very intelligent, friendly, and relaxed person.

[. . .] I remember classmates collecting signatures and joining democratic student movements to protest against fascism. Amílcar was also part of these anti-fascist student committees. Later, when there were meetings, he always distinguished himself. He spoke very well; he was the one who always managed things.

[. . .] From the second to the third year, in October 1948, only twenty-five of us passed the course. Thus, there was only one class group.

Amílcar dedicated himself conscientiously to his studies and also expanded the scope of his general knowledge. A poem dated 1946 reveals his concerns at the time:

. . . No, poetry:
Don't hide in the caves of my being, don't
run away from Life.

Break the invisible bars of my prison, open
wide the doors of my being
—and come out . . .

Come out to struggle (life is a struggle)
the men outside call for you,
and you, Poetry, are also a Man.

Who loves Poems from all over the World,
—who loves Men;
Release your poems for all races, for all things.
Confuse your body with all the bodies in the world,
confuse yourself with me . . .

Go, Poetry:
Take my arms to embrace the World, give me
your arms to embrace Life. My Poetry is me.[33]

As is easy to understand, the identity established between being and poetry is not a gratuitous image.

What did Amílcar Cabral think and produce? What was his universe in these student years? We know through several testimonies from his contemporaries and the correspondence exchanged with Maria Helena. Amílcar dedicated a particularly dear poem to her, the "Sonnet of our Love."[34]

About it, he wrote:

> Fonseca [probably Aguinaldo Fonseca], the Cape Verdean poet I told you about, read the sonnet and said to me: "I would just like to meet the woman who, with Life, inspires you to do a work like this."

> And, paradoxically, he added: "I congratulate you on your unhappiness; you come out well in everything: football, study, prose, verse, etc."[35]

At this time, a pressing appeal, if not an obsession, came from the deepest part of his consciousness: the return to Africa.

> ... But you know, as I do, the forces that call me to Africa, forces that I will not resist, because to do so would be betraying myself and betraying life itself.[36]

He affirmed his deep love for his family, in which "all the benevolent and affectionate light that comes from my mother is reflected," and added:

> But that is not what draws me to Africa, especially since, day by day, I become more convinced that I won't go to Cape Verde. What calls me are millions of individuals who need my contribution in the thankless struggle they have

been waging with Nature and with men. What calls me is Humanity itself, requesting—better yet, demanding—that I fulfill my duty as a Man. And everything tells me, everything tells me that my job, at least initially, is there. There, where, despite the progressive and beautiful cities on the coast, there are still thousands of beings (human beings) who live in complete darkness.

There, where Technique and Science are still shadows, where Nature, rich in secrets, virgin of riches and secrets, offers those who want to work and do something for Men, the most interesting reasons with regard to the profession that we have chosen. There, where life calls me, where I will have live part of my life because life itself needs me.[37]

Amílcar was preparing to travel a long path whose contours were being progressively outlined. And he was sharpening his weapons: work, fulfilling his duties as a student, intellectual culture. His deepest desire was to clarify, study, and build. At the beginning of 1949, he wrote these memorable lines:

I have lived life intensely, and from that life, I bring experiences that have given me a direction, a path that I have to follow, no matter how great the personal losses it may demand.

This is the reason for my life.[38]

Amílcar certainly lived an intense life divided between the Institute of Agronomy, the Casa dos Estudantes do Império [House of the Students of the Empire] where he was an activist, and the reading that was opening his mind to an understanding of the world.

Among the books that were spreading among the narrow circle of African students was the *Anthologie de la nouvelle poésie nègre et malgache* [Anthology of New Black and Malagasy Poetry] by Léopold Sédar Senghor.[39] Amílcar expressed his boundless enthusiasm when learning about these poems in the following terms:

Things I never even dreamed of, wonderful poems written by black people from all parts of the French world, poems talking about Africa, about slaves, about men, about the lives and aspirations of men.

Sublime . . . infinitely human . . .

This book has given me a lot and, among many things, the certainty that the Black man, the much-exploited Black man, is waking up all over the world. And it is not a selfish awakening, like so many that History talks about. No. It is a universal awakening, with open arms for all Men of good will. Without hate, but with love, a love such as only slavery can establish in the soul of a human being. Because, as Jean-Paul Sartre said, *"la négritude n'est pas un état* [. . . *(elle)] est amour* [blackness is not a state, it is love].["](#)[40]

Attentive as always to issues related to the problems of the Cape Verde islands, Amílcar Cabral passed up no opportunity to discuss and argue, in a word, to reflect, and beyond that, *to convince.* How can we consider Cape Verdeans at that time? Or, in other words, how can the Cape Verdean personality be defined?

In his comment on an article published in the newspaper *Comércio do Porto,* he affirms the existence of a Cape Verdean people whom he regards as the result of the merger of the archipelago's first inhabitants and accepts that before the arrival of the Portuguese navigators, the islands were not inhabited by any indigenous people in the strict sense of the term. He continued his reflection to demonstrate that nature has certainly not managed to homogenize the Cape Verdean man from a physical point of view, that is, in terms of skin color and anthropomorphic features and characteristics. But there is an increasingly marked tendency towards this homogeneity, which confirmed the statistical indications from the population census: the number of mestizos, resulting from the fusion of blacks and whites, is six times higher than that of whites and three times higher than that of blacks. From a psychic point of view, no one can deny the existence of a "Cape Verdean spirit" that defines the *caboverdianidade.*

Beyond the discussion about this regional specificity, Cabral formulates clear ideas on a more general level:

> It is not the existence of a race or an ethnic group or anything else that defines or conditions the behavior of a human group. No. Instead, it is the social environment and the problems resulting from the reaction to that environment and the reactions of the men involved in it. All of this defines their behavior. Put another way: a group of men—human beings—will make up a "race" or "ethnic group" or something else, insofar as they face common problems and struggle for common aspirations.[41]

He begins to better understand the concepts that will later become the driving force and justification for his life: the concept of *liberation*.

According to his point of view, man, once equipped with the modern achievements of science, more than ever enjoys the possibility of realizing his model or project of civilization, that is, freeing himself from the determinism of his condition of an animal by dominating nature or making use of it: satisfying his needs—needs inherent to all men—by protecting himself against the evils of the planet and using all the advantages of progress that man has achieved for all men. For him, "civilization will be the set of social, moral, and economic characteristics that come closest to this objective, always leaving the path open to evolution, to transformations likely to better achieve that which is good for men."[42]

Cabral set out on a mission not only to listen to, but also to bring about the aspirations of men:* firstly, those of his archipelago, an integral part of the African continent.

Putting his profession of poetic faith in harmony with his militant behavior, Cabral decided to spend his school holidays on the islands, to "awaken Cape Verdean public opinion against Portuguese colonialism."

The end of summer and the beginning of autumn 1949 effectively marked an important stage in his development as a propagator of lib-

---

* Andrade means this not in the gendered sense, although contemporarily we would certainly prefer the use of the term "humans."

erating ideas. Having perfectly mastered his technical specialty—soil erosion—he dedicated himself to making Cape Verde known to Cape Verdeans themselves.

This was an ambitious project that should have been completed in September and October: two months of feverish activity, interrupted by illness.[43]

The presence of Amílcar Cabral in Praia and beyond the capital, throughout the archipelago, was noted through a lecture read out on the Rádio-Clube de Cabo Verde, under the title "Some Considerations About the Rains." This was a scientific commentary on a tangible fact, observable by the population: the return of the rains in the early hours of August 18. Cabral summed up the change in attitude caused by this phenomenon and extracts its underlying meaning: the Cape Verdean people would recognize that, despite all the obstacles, agriculture was the basis of its economy, hence the need to understand how to build a life on the islands in which the specter of hunger does not constantly assail the spirits. It was therefore necessary to elucidate, clarify, and raise consciousness in the *man of the street* "to remind him of the realities that condition his life, integrating him little by little into the system of life that, abandoning misfortune, is subordinated to a sense of prevention, so that every useful element can be found to guard against the uncertainties of the future." He ended these prudent considerations by professing hope in the destiny of the people of Cape Verde:

> Because, if it is true, as the History of the Peoples demonstrates, that hunger was the initiator of Progress, there are few people who have more right to Progress than Cape Verdeans. Because, if it is true, as Plato, the unsurpassed sage, said, that necessity is the mother of our engines, no people, more than the Cape Verdean, has the right and the duty to find the "engines" indispensable to the meeting your needs.[44]

The governor of the colony, Alves Roçadas, wrote on the card acknowledging receipt of this text: "Together, we will carry the cross to Calvary with greater satisfaction."[45]

Cabral had to accelerate the pace of his work, making the most of the time allocated to him by the Radio's management. He returned to the issue of agriculture in another comment, regarding an article published in *Diário Popular*:

> The Cape Verde archipelago is a rich territory with great industrial possibilities. It is from its own wealth that it must organize its economy.

Now is the right moment to deal with the relationship between the earth and man and to talk about agricultural resources and varieties. But it is above all the moment chosen to pose the problem of the *élite* in society: its role in eliminating the people's conditions of backwardness, with a view to leading them on the path of progress.

> This is why in every society there is an *élite* (an intellectual and not a class *élite*) whose proper function is and must be to enlighten the majority, helping them to achieve an increasingly better standard of living for themselves, without that same majority ever being betrayed.

> Now the question arises: In Cape Verde, is there such a real, tangible *élite*? There are undoubtedly elements of affirmed value but, in our view, these need an amalgam of efforts to direct their activity towards the masses.[46]

Cabral claims that the *intellectual vanguard* of the population has the moral obligation to provide ordinary Cape Verdeans with exact knowledge of their problems. Or, in his own terms: "The cadres must enlighten those who are in ignorance."

This knowledge of problems is not limited to the narrow space of the archipelago but extends to the entire world. This is the reason why the radio programs addressed the realities of the islands of Fogo and São Vicente, as well as the music of black Americans and Brazilian culture.

From all these texts comes the conviction and determination that encouraged their author to carry out the militant task of *raising the consciousness* of the broadest layers of the Cape Verdean people. According to Amílcar Cabral himself, one month after their launch, the colonial authorities banned the programs.

> It was interesting to note that in Praia, for example, people gathered in large numbers in the public square to ask for the program to continue. But the Portuguese banned the program. The governor also refused a request we made in 1949 to give night classes to any adults who were interested at the Escola Central da Praia. They asked us what the program was, we showed it to them. In accordance with the wishes of the authorities, it was for the people of Cape Verde to get to know Cape Verde. They refused.[47]

Cabral used a recently appeared national newspaper to present a study on the central problem of soil erosion, in a series of articles that he began writing in Praia in September 1949 and concluded in Lisbon in October of the following year.

As a starting point and conclusion of these writings, [he wrote on] the decision on the need for change: "What is necessary is for Cape Verde to be reborn through the work of man."[48]

It deals with the issue of erosion, traces its history, diagnoses the causes, analyzes the effects, and finally, proposes solutions to eliminate it or at least avoid it. This is the central axis of his ideas: "Defending the soil is the most effective process to defend man."

Cabral, who continues to be haunted by the drama of the drought, welcomes the return of the rains in a poem entitled *"Regresso"*:

A chuva amiga, Mamãi Velha, a chuva,
que há tanto tempo não batia assim . . .
Ouvi dizer que a Cidade-Velha,
—a Ilha toda—
Em poucos dias já virou jardim . . .

Dizem que o campo se cobriu de verde,
da cor mais bela, porque é a cor da esp'rança. Que a terra, agora,

é mesmo CABO VERDE.
—E a tempestade que virou bonança . . . *

On balance, his stay in the archipelago had been largely positive and the experience proved decisive for the immediate future. As he began his last university year (1949–50), Cabral and all of his colleagues worked on a yearbook which celebrated, in the joyful and light tone that is specific to this particular academic tradition, the end of his studies at the Instituto Superior de Agronomia. He signed the opening poem: "*O adeus à Tapada*," a salutation of recognition tempered with a note of nostalgia for the institution where the weapons that would allow young engineers to enter life were forged.

On the page reserved for him, Amílcar Cabral wrote these verses dedicated to his mother:

> *Para ti, Mãe Iva,*
> *Eu deixo uma parcela*
> *Do meu livro de curso.*
> *P'ra ti, que foste a estrela*
> *Da minha infância agreste.*
> *P'ra ti, Mãe, que me deste*
> *A tua alma viva*
> *E o teu Amor profundo,*
> *Maior que o próprio Mundo!*
>
> *Aceita este tributo,*
> *Que tudo quanto eu for,*
> *Será do teu Amor,*
> *—Tua carne, Mãe, teu fruto!*

---

* The friendly rain, Mamãi Velha, the rain,
which hadn't fallen like this for so long . . .
I heard that Cidade-Velha,
—the whole island—
In just a few days became a garden . . .

They say the fields were covered in green,
the most beautiful color, because it is the color of hope.
That the land, now, really is THE GREEN CAPE.
—And the storm became a cornucopia . . .

Sem ti, não sou ninguém.
Só sou—porque és Mãe.**

There was another significant innovation in the yearbook: on the page bearing the caricature of Cabral, Alda do Espírito Santo (outside the Institute) could be seen prophesying about him in a song full of hope.

From time to time, Cabral composed other verses for various colleagues as a way of expressing his active sympathy.

❖ ❖ ❖ ❖ ❖

Make the reality of the archipelago known to Cape Verdeans themselves . . . This first step in the political-cultural pedagogy that Cabral undertook in Santiago in 1949 found echoes in a similar movement taking place in Luanda at the time. *Vamos descobrir Angola* [Let's discover Angola] was launched by a group of young intellectuals who formed the entourage of the poet Viriato da Cruz.

Meanwhile, the collective commitment of a handful of men was being tempered in political battles taking place in the colonial-fascist center of Lisbon. Since enrolling at the university, Cabral had formed close connections with groups of students from the various Portuguese colonies.

Due to their class origins, these students perforce came from the modest popular strata of the urban petite bourgeoisie that colonial legislation designated by the idiotic term *assimilados* [the assimilated]. The more conscious among them had been sensitized by the tangible reality of colonial exploitation suffered by the popular masses—and

** For you, Mother Iva,
I leave a part
Of my yearbook.
For you, who were the star
Of my rustic childhood.
For you, Mother, who gave me
Your living soul
And your deep Love,
Bigger than the World itself!

Accept this tribute, Because
Everything that I may become,
Will be born from your Love,
—Your flesh, Mother, your fruit!

Without you, I'm nobody.
I only am—because you are Mother.

by the students themselves—and, to a lesser extent, by the effects of that exploitation in their own material and social lives. Those who had made it to the university, generally thanks to enormous financial sacrifices made by their families, as well as the selective game of university places reserved for *assimilados*, bore the stigma of revolt. Their awareness of the negation of the colonized was derived from their objective material conditions and from the aggression that they had suffered in their cultural personalities as Africans. Armed with the privilege of education, these *assimilados* found themselves confronted with a dilemma: Should they struggle for self-promotion within the framework of colonial society? Or should they arm themselves culturally to contest and destroy the system of domination? In other words, they faced a choice between two conceptions of life: individual ascension through accepting the laws of the system—or else a global refusal; in short, a rupture that would open the way to liberation of the strata most oppressed by colonialism. The definition of nationalist unity in the Portuguese colonies, the content of their ideology, and the form in which their fight would take place were progressively developed and refined around these ideas. At this early stage, we still find ourselves on the threshold of 1950. The number of intellectuals capable of speaking the liberating language of *la bouche des malheurs qui n'ont point de bouches* [the mouth of sufferings which have no mouth], in the words of the poet Aimé Césaire, was pitifully small.

Nonetheless, this handful of African students in Portugal was engaged in feverish activity on two complementary planes: firstly, ideological and political training, expressed by the acquisition of knowledge across all domains in meetings that were all, to some degree, clandestine, and through reading Marx and a range of other works that discussed progressive social ideas. The logical outcome of this was active participation in Portuguese youth and democratic organizations, such as Movimento de Unidade Democrática (MUD) Juvenil and Movimento da Paz. Secondly, the safeguarding of their identity or, as Cabral put it, the struggle for the "re-Africanization of minds." As the students became acutely aware of their specific situation as colonized and assimilated subjects, they rationalized their feelings, looking for African cultural practices that could be revitalized, and opened up to knowledge of similar experiences forged in the universe of oppression. Thus, they absorbed the ideas of the North

American "new negro" and the negritude movement in the French colonial empire that they learned about through Léopold Sédar Senghor's famous anthology, the contacts that they established with the journal *Présence Africaine*, and their quest for information on the evolution of political struggles in Africa. Agostinho Neto expressed this moment of certainty in one of his first poems:

. . . .

Enquanto o sorriso brilhava no canto de dor
e as mãos construíam mundos maravilhosos John foi linchado
o irmão chicoteado nas costas nuas a mulher amordaçada
e o filho continuou ignorante

E do drama intenso duma vida imensa e útil resultou certeza
As minhas mãos colocaram pedras nos alicerces do mundo
mereço o meu pedaço de pão.[49,*]

It was not enough for the deep search for African identity to be limited to the simple level of individual awareness or solitary reading: its natural extension was found in bringing together the diverse elements of the African community in Portugal, while at the same time establishing permanent contacts with the core of political organizations that was developing in Portugal's colonies.

At the time, there was an organization known as Casa de África, founded by an old man from São Tomé, Raul de Castro, a journalist oscillating between obedience to the Ministry of Colonies and to nationalism, but whose natural tendency leaned towards the defense of his interests on the side of the Portuguese. Castro had some fundings and an existing organizational structure that the nationalists

---

*   While the smile shone
    in the corner of pain
    and hands built wonderful worlds
    John was lynched
    the brother's bare back flogged
    the wife gagged
    and the son not knowing

    And from the intense drama
    of an immense and useful life
    resulted certainty
    My hands laid stones
    on the foundations of the world
    I deserve my piece of bread.

intended to take over with a view toward making it the base for their activities. Several meetings with Castro took place. He was suspicious (rightly, from his point of view) of the political uses that young nationalists wanted to make of his institution.[50]

Dozens of Africans demonstrated in the Casa da África, which was located in the center of Lisbon, and demanded that control over it be ceded to them. Throughout the night, old Castro held out against their demands. Then, in the midst of the tumult, Amílcar Cabral stood up and addressed the crowd, saying: "All the honest Africans here should leave now!" And so they did. Upon arriving on the street, they were confronted with the shadows of fascist order. They were quickly dispersed. This episode marked the end of their contacts with Raul de Castro. From the historical point of view, this may well have been the first time that Cabral's ability to inspire men to action became evident.

African sailors employed by shipping companies, known in Portuguese as *embarcadiços* [shipworkers] and who suffered fierce exploitation and racial discrimination, turned out to play a key connecting role. They were members of the Clube Marítimo, located in the Lisbon neighborhood of Graça, where the student group engaged in political and cultural activities targeted at them.[51] *Embarcadiços* like Zito Van Dunem conveyed messages to and picked up instructions and information from African ports and imported subversive books from Brazil. António Domingues captured this period in his portraits and other paintings.

Following their unsuccessful attempt to co-opt the Casa da África, the students set up their own Centro de Estudos Africanos [African Studies Center].[52] Its work fell under six fields divided into several subfields: (I) The Earth and Man; (II) African Socio-Economy; (III) Black Thought; (IV) The Problems of the Portuguese Overseas Empire; (V) The Black Man in the World; (VI) Fundamental Problems for the Progress of the Black World. According to the organizer's directives, each field was to be discussed in seminar format. Meetings took place on Sundays at the home of the Espírito Santo family, originally from São Tomé, at 37 Rua Actor Vale.

Today, rereading documents from the time, preserved in spite of furious secret police searches and relentless criticism from rats of all kinds, we can date the first meeting of the African Studies Center as having taken place in October 1951 (we can be sure, in any case, that Francisco José Tenreiro participated for the first time on October 21). Cabral delivered lectures on the themes of "Land use: cultivations systems, Black African characteristics. Advantages and disadvantages of shifting cultivation." In spite of its formal aspect as a place for conferences, followed by debate, the African Studies Center transformed itself into a locus for the meeting and melding of the progressive ideas that were stirring the African community.

The collective contribution from many of the main actors at the Center to *Présence Africaine* on the subject of students in the world was the first example of the Center making itself heard beyond the frontiers of the Portuguese empire.[53] Another initiative of the Center in Lisbon was the modest publication of the first *Caderno de poesia negra de expressão portuguesa [Journal of Black Poetry in the Portuguese Language].*[54] The close police surveillance exercised over the Espírito Santo family after the massacres in São Tomé during the tragic days of February 1953, forced the sessions being held at the Center to be suspended.* They then resumed and lasted until April 11, 1954.

Cultural concerns were progressively opened up to political organization. At this point the hierarchy of values between Portuguese democratic groups and organizational autonomy became evident. Many of the African students were still involved in such Portuguese entities as MUD Juvenil and Movimento da Paz, where they represented the colonial peoples, but an objective political analysis led to the conclusion that it was necessary to break with the static notion of the reciprocity of consequences between the struggle against fascism and the struggle against colonialism.

---

* Andrade here refers to the Batepá Massacre where Portuguese colonists and militias massacred hundreds of Sao Tomeans who protested the colonial policy of forced labor. The Portuguese falsely attributed the protests to "communist agitation."

THREE

Return to the Home Country

Having finished his university studies at the end of the 1949–50 school year with the high grade of 15 out of a possible 16, Amílcar Cabral completed internships the following year as an agricultural engineer and a colonial agricultural engineer, once again receiving high grades: 18 out of a possible 19.[55]

While a trainee member of the soil brigade at the Santarém agricultural station, he learned of the death of his father, Juvenal Cabral. This news greatly affected him. Having made the political decision to return to Guinea some time ago, he headed for Bissau in 1952, as an employee of the Provincial Division of Agricultural and Forestry Services in Portuguese Guinea.

This was the starting point for a new phase that would be decisive for the future. When Cabral disembarked in his native country at the age of twenty-eight, he appeared to his compatriots as a man determined to fight major political battles. An African shaped in the crucible of an insular region of the continent, a survivor of the tragedy of hunger, perfectly educated in the dual nature of the Portuguese regime—in the colonies and in the metropolis—his contemporaries saw him as tasked with raising the awareness of the popular masses in the concrete conditions of Guinea-Bissau.

> After the last world war, the need to struggle to end colonial domination began to grow in people's consciousness. At that time, a group of students from the Portuguese colonies who were studying in Lisbon, began to think about

how to become Africans again, because the Portuguese's trick was always to let us be not Africans but instead second-class Portuguese. Whenever someone was lucky enough to attend school, the Portuguese counted on him as an agent who would deny Africa to serve the colonialists. At that time, our work was to rediscover our African roots, and it was so good, so useful and consequential, and had so many consequences, that today, the founders of that group in Lisbon are all leading the liberation movements in the Portuguese colonies . . .

Then, piecemeal, we started returning to our countries, finding other people who thought the same way as us, we began to look for a way to awaken everyone's spirit and the desire for freedom. It was very difficult.

We didn't go to Guinea-Bissau by chance, nor for any material need—everything was thought out and calculated step by step. We had enormous possibilities because we could be anywhere in the other Portuguese colonies, or even in Portugal itself, as we had left a good position at the Estação Agronómica de Lisboa, as researchers, to find a place as second-class agricultural engineers in Guinea-Bissau.

[. . .] Therefore, it was calculated. The idea was to do something, to make a contribution, to uplift the people and struggle against the Portuguese. And that is just what we did that from the first day we set foot in Guinea.[56]

Cabral's political aim was clear but he still needed to discover the social terrain of the struggle.

Rarely has an African revolutionary been as well-placed as "The Engineer" (as Cape Verdeans liked to call him) to create a means to change the socioeconomic realities of the towns and the countryside. Amílcar Cabral immediately made contact with his former high school classmates and realized that only a small number of Cape Verdeans, by virtue of their social position, were ever likely to join a nationalist organization. He experimented with a method of mobilization that involved using his personal influence at his workplace (Granja de Pessubé) and favoring an atmosphere of African fraternity through parties. When Cape Verdeans are invited to take a stand, to put themselves in the footprints of the oppressed and commit to concrete action, they tended to step back. Nonetheless, some did follow The Engineer: Aristides Pereira, Júlio de Almeida, Fernando Fortes, and Abilio Duarte. Cabral summed the problem of the moment—the struggle for national independence—and appealed to Cape Verdeans to join the Guineans and bring about the failure of the Portuguese colonialists' efforts to divide the two communities. He expanded the field of his contacts and organized meetings in the poor Bissau neighborhoods of Pélon and Chão dos Papeis. Infiltrators reported the meetings to the police. "Subversive" issues were in fact being discussed, such as an attack on a governor.

And when, he said in 1954 or almost at the end of 1953, if I'm not mistaken, Governor Serrão was going to be replaced and there was a rumor that his successor in Guinea-Bissau would be Gorgulho (that assassin who had the troops and settlers in São Tomé kill one thousand Santomeans in a matter of days), we decided, in a meeting in Pélon, to kill Gorgulho on the pier, on the very day he arrived. The man who was to have killed him was our comrade Bacar Cassamá, who is now in charge of the Party and is in the Bafatá area.[57]

But all this agitation did not affect his work as an agronomist in any way. Since 1953, Cabral had been assigned the job of planning and executing Guinea's agricultural census. He carried out this task with such competence and professional awareness that his report continues to be referred even today as the first source of comprehensive information about Guinean agriculture. He had the opportunity to understand the structures of economic exploitation in depth, from the roots up, and in scientific terms. Through contact with farmers, he was able to understand the social and cultural data of the ethnic groups of Guinea (the things that divided them and those that united them) and to identify the essential foundations of the motivations for the struggle against colonial domination.[58]

Cabral also gave advice about the use of *legal space*. And he gave the starting signal by writing, in 1954, the statutes for the constitution of the Associação Desportiva, Recreativa, e Cultural da Guiné [Sporting, Recreational and Cultural Association of Guinea], or the

Sporting Club. The text provides for the right of admission for all Guineans without discrimination, be they: *indigenous, "uncivilized,"* or *"assimilated."* However, as most of the signatories who deposited the club's statutes do not have identity cards, the Portuguese civil administration formally rejected them and the club was therefore not authorized to operate. Finally, the governor of the colony, frigate captain Diogo de Melo e Alvim, expressed his concern and had a long explanatory conversation with Cabral. According to his brother Luís, the dialogue between the two men began more or less as follows:

The Governor: So, you're the head of the local Mau-Mau?

Cabral: As far as I know, there aren't any Mau-Mau in Guinea. The Mau-Mau are in Kenya.

The Governor: Very well, then. Look, Mr. Engineer, live your life, be a man of your time, but don't screw my career.[59]

The governor forced Cabral to leave Guinea but authorized him to return once a year to visit his family.

It was 1955, the year of the Bandung Conference. The first conference of the peoples of Africa and Asia, in which the great leaders of what was not yet the Third World took part: Nasser, Zhou Enlai, Nehru . . . In Asia, Vietnam's first war of independence had ended the previous year with the victory of Dien Bien Phu, which felt like a victory for all oppressed people. In Africa, only a few months earlier, the Algerian FLN (National Liberation Front) had begun an armed insurrection . . .

The administrative measure that had been taken against Amílcar Cabral allowed him to enrich his scientific and political experience. That same year he would be working with two of his former soil technology professors and as the head of the agrological studies brigade of the Cassequel Agricultural Society in Angola. During his time in Angola, between visits and missions, The Engineer (Cabral) actively participated in the emergence of the political formations that would go on to become the MPLA (People's Movement for the Liberation of Angola). Present on two battlefields (not forgetting his time on the island of São Tomé), he then dedicated his life and work to developing the strategy for the unitary struggle against Portuguese colonialism.

Particularly in Bissau, Bafatá, and Bolama, the first group of Guinean militants began disseminating patriotic propaganda and infiltrating legal associations.[60]

Thus, in mid-1956, agitation began among commercial and industrial employees (in the squares and in the countryside) in order to prepare a true union movement. This was about putting an end to the inversion of values then prevailing in the Sindicato dos Empregados do Comércio e da Indústria da Guiné [Trade and Industry Employees Union of Guinea]. The leadership of the union included European employees in high positions and, as an exception to the union's general rule, one or two Cape Verdeans who practiced a liberal profession. In reality, all employees were union members and as such had to pay a monthly fee of around twenty *escudos*, but they did not have a shop steward.

The chairman of the General Council of the union and its first secretary were directly appointed by the governor. In reality, the union functioned as a labor recruitment office. It controlled employee records with a view to informing employers about the availability of staff for companies. It accumulated employee contributions but did not guarantee them any kind of social protection. There was a rumor that the union trafficked in funds transfers and loans, while abuses of all kinds were rife: there was no job security, salary tables were routinely violated, arbitrary dismissals were common currency. A group of patriots decided to struggle for control of the union to turn the situation around: Luís Cabral, head of accounting at the Gouveia company; Abílio Duarte, clerk at Banco Nacional Ultramarino; João Rosa,[61] SCOA (Sociedade Comercial Oeste-Africana) employee; Elisée Turpin, employed by NOSOCO (Nova Sociedade Comercial); and Victor Robalo, farmer. They succeeded in taking over the leadership of the union, but their victory was short-lived.[62]

This primitive battle reinforced the patriots in their conviction that only the existence of a *political* and *clandestine* mechanism would allow them to effectively confront the repressive machine of colonialism and see the aspirations of the popular masses triumph. Neither the MING (Movement for the Independence of Guinea), created and disappeared in 1955, nor the MLG (Movement for the Liberation of

Guinea), each with very restricted audiences, were capable of offering a response to this objective.

After taking stock of the country's general situation with his first traveling companions during a brief stay in Bissau, Amílcar Cabral chaired a meeting during which a *historic* decision was made: to form the Partido Africano da Independência—União dos Povos da Guiné e Cabo Verde (African Independence Party—Union of the Peoples of Guinea and Cape Verde). Six people were present at the meeting: Amílcar Cabral, Aristides Pereira, Luís Cabral, Júlio de Almeida, Fernando Fortes, and Elisée Turpin. The meeting took place at dusk on September 19, 1956, at 9C Rua Guerra Junqueiro.[63] The line adopted by the party was as follows:

> The time has come to prepare our people to take on a decisive era in its history, that of the struggle for national liberation, which will only triumph through the mobilization of all the children of our homelands without distinction of sex, tribe, or color. It will be the struggle of all Guineans and Cape Verdeans dedicated to the pursuit of happiness for all the children of these two countries. However, to engage in this struggle, our people need leadership. The party must be organized in a clandestine manner to evade colonial police surveillance.

This party—the PAI[64]—the significance of whose strategy in the historical context of his time we will later examine, acted within the scope of the strictest secrecy. As its existence was only known exclusively to party members, no written trace of the date of its appearance could be found, either inside or outside the borders of Guinea-Bissau and Cape Verde.[65]

The PAI emerged on the political scene at a time when the African situation (and the Sékou Touré government) allowed for its general secretariat to be established in Guinea-Conakry.

What was Amílcar Cabral doing during the four years between the founding of the party and its external delegation being set up in Conakry? He continued to carry out his duties as the head of the phytosanitary protection and agrological studies brigades, which led to a series of trips between Portugal, Angola, and Guinea-Bissau. Cabral made a brief stay in Paris, in November 1957, to participate in the "Consultation and Study Meeting for the Development of the Struggle Against Portuguese Colonialism." He then revived the anticolonialist flame in Lisbon, and made a discreet visit to the Ghanian capital of Accra, where the first Pan-African conference took place. He then headed to Luanda, where he learned of the Pidjiguiti massacre.

He returned to Bissau in September 1959 to preside for the last time over an important PAIGC meeting.* January 1960 saw him in Tunis for the Second Conference of African Peoples. Next stop was in London, where he wrote a pamphlet entitled "Facts about Portuguese Colonialism."[66] His final port of call for the year was Conakry in May. The establishment of the PAIGC's external secretariat in Conakry signaled an intense period of activity for Amílcar Cabral. This period, 1960–62, preceding the outbreak of the armed struggle, saw him focus on three key areas:

I. Training Activists as the Intermediate Cadres Essential for Disseminating Party Ideas within the Country

The Conakry base welcomed a significant number of young people from the outskirts of the urban centers and the countryside, most of whom already belonged to the Party. Others followed the same path. Surrounded by a handful of key leaders, Cabral personally directed a program that aimed both at educating cadres and providing them with the political and ideological foundations necessary to carry out the tasks of popular mobilization. This process took on particular importance after February 4, 1961, when the MPLA began its inevitable transition to armed struggle.

II. Consolidate the PAIGC Position in Neighboring Countries

Party and state leaders in Guinea-Conakry and Senegal tended to make use of emigrant groups from so-called Portuguese Guinea as an additional political force and as a docile clientele. Amílcar Cabral found himself having to explain to representatives of the Touré government the opportunistic nature of the campaigns led by the enemies of the PAIGC and Guinea-Conakry's PDG (Democratic Party of

---

* This meeting was in direct response to the Pidjiguiti Massacre of August 3 1959. It was here where Cabral gave the directive to move away from labor actions, and nonviolent civil disobedience, and for party cadre to go to rural Guinea where they would win over prepare the population for armed struggle against Portuguese colonialism.

Guinea—African Democratic Rally). Undoubtedly, without the prior independence of Guinea-Conakry, the history of the PAIGC would have been entirely different. Things were harder in Senegal, where elements within the national leadership advocated boycotting or even eliminating the PAIGC. Later, they would have to adjust to reality.

Amílcar Cabral had a clear-eyed understanding of the situation:

> We had plenty of reasons to be angry with our brothers in Guinea-Conakry. Remember when they arrested all our comrades who were in Conakry? Everyone was waiting for the struggle to start within our country, and our people were all arrested. But we knew how to implement the necessary policy, not only how to get our people out of the dungeon, but to further strengthen our friendship with and the trust of our brothers from the Guinea-Conakry. For six years, we fought the hostility coming from Senegal but in the end, they recognized our Party. This was a great victory in our struggle. You can imagine, therefore, the struggle that we are engaged in. I hope no one thinks that we could have won the internal battle without winning the external one. It may be true that rice is cooked inside a pot. But to cook it you need fire and the fire is outside the pot.

> In the concrete conditions of the lives of the people of our country, it would not be possible to carry out the struggle in Guinea-Bissau—we have to say this clearly—if we had not achieved the victories that we achieved abroad, especially in these two neighboring countries, and particularly in Guinea-Conakry.[67]

III. Obtain International Support

The PAIGC, like the MPLA, had just participated for the first time in a Pan-African assembly held in Tunis in January 1960. The PAIGC and the MPLA defined their unitary strategy within the framework of FRAIN (Frente Revolucionária Africana para a Independência Nacional das Colónias Portuguesas [African Revolutionary Front for the National Independence of the Portuguese Colonies]).[68] From Conakry, their leaders could send requests for support to countries that could provide it in the spirit of combative solidarity: *socialist* countries. The historical truth demands that we remember that in August 1960, the People's Republic of China was the first to welcome a joint mission from the MPLA and the PAIGC and then granted them both relatively substantial aid. Amílcar Cabral headed his party's delegation, accompanied by young cadres who remained in China to begin preparation for guerrilla warfare and perfect their ideological training.[69]

Later, the founding of CONCP (Conferência das Organizações Nacionalistas das Colónias Portuguesas [Conference of Nationalist Organizations of the Portuguese Colonies]) on April 18, 1961 in Casablanca, thanks to the decisive support of the Kingdom of Morocco, expanded the possibilities of acquiring multifaceted support on an international scale.[70]

The founding of the PAIGC was situated within the historical context of its time: the events of the period immediately after the end of the war and the decade of 1951–60, which certainly constituted the most decisive phase for the African continent in the development of modern ideas for freedom and progress among the masses. The postwar period, which reflected a new relationship of forces at an international level, was dominated by the feats of arms unfolding in Asia which would accelerate the process of African emancipation. These events acquired a universal scope: the victory of the army of national liberation, which led to the proclamation of the People's Republic of China and the *revolutionary armed struggle* led by the Việt Minh which, after the defeat of French colonial troops in Dien Bien Phu, gave rise to the Democratic Republic of Vietnam. Kwame Nkrumah's "Appeal to Oppressed Peoples," while not widely known outside the British colonies, was made at the end of the Fifth Pan-African Congress held in Manchester from October 12 to October 15, 1945, and revealed a considerable degree of anti-imperialist consistency.

Formulated here for the first time was *the preliminary demand to immediate and unconditional political independence.* Nationalist forces took advantage of the liberal gaps in the imperialist metropolises to build parties with a unitary vocation. This was the case for the Rassemblement Démocratique Africane [established] on October 19, 1946 in Bamako, and the Istiqlal and Neo-Destour parties, [established] in Morocco and Tunisia.

But European liberalism also engaged in bloody repression, such as the 1947 Madagascar massacres. However, none of the colonial metropolises of Great Britain, France, and Belgium (the main imperialist powers) were run by a dictatorial regime with fascist characteristics, which was the case of Portugal. From the Suez Canal to the shores of the Indian Ocean, African popular forces definitively entered into combat against foreign exploiters.

The decade 1951–60 successively recorded the Mau-Mau war (October 1952), the creation of the Republic of Egypt (1952–53), and the outbreak of the insurrection in Algeria on November 1, 1954.

And then, on April 18, 1955, the thunder of Bandung tore forever the veil between Africa and Asia. As Joseph Ki-Zerbo wrote of the first "Estates General" of oppressed peoples: until then, across twenty-nine countries, a billion men who had been mere objects now intended to become subjects.

The wheel of history was accelerating its pace everywhere. The political events occurring at breakneck speed in the heart of the continent were realizations of the African peoples' aspirations to take their destinies into their own hands. The leaders expressed the determination to *reconquer* the African personality on all levels—a movement that Cabral would later call the *return to history*. The imperialist powers tried to take over these peoples' initiatives and organizations, being quite willing to grant formal independence. The process of neocolonialism was beginning.

But Africa was united by its poles of resistance: Egypt nationalized the Suez Canal and challenged the Franco-British imperialist alliance; Ghana revived Pan-Africanism; Guinea-Conakry dared to radically reject the French neocolonial dependence proposed by General De Gaulle; Algeria reinforced the armed struggle for national liberation; the people of Cameroon were fighting under their great leader Um Nyobè.

Meanwhile, in the African American region of Cuba, men also triumphed in a guerrilla war that would turn into a revolution. Finally, the successive assemblies of progressive organizations and independent states held in Cairo and Accra constituted, for the nascent nationalist movements in Angola, Guinea-Bissau, and Congo, the reference points of Pan-Africanism and Afro-Asianism.

From the time he entered university in 1945 in Lisbon, until the eve of the armed struggle in Guinea-Bissau, seventeen years had passed. During these years, Amílcar Cabral forged the most important instrument of liberation for his people, the *Party*. And he had become what he would be until his death: *the convener of men.*

Part II.
The Weapon of Criticism and the Instruments of Knowledge

FOUR

The Formation of Cabral's Political Thought

I. The Scientific Basis. Analysis of Works on Agriculture in Guinea: The Socio-Political Dimension

The formation of Amílcar Cabral's political thought appears clearly when we consider the historical context of his time, the institutions he faced, and the action he was led to undertake. Armed with his agronomic engineering degree from a period of brilliant studies as we have just seen, Cabral had achieved, in the country where he was born, dual tasks in the work of a militant: understanding, through his technical knowledge, the concrete realities of the Guinean people and laying the foundations for organizing the political struggle against colonial domination. His abundant output—consisting of notes, studies, reports, and, above all, the agricultural census—confirms the way in which he fulfilled the first aspect of that immense task. One day, experts will, without a doubt, subject Cabral's vast scientific bibliography to a profound examination. Cabral equally utilized his skills as an agronomist at the service of other countries: he actively collaborated in research missions on coffee and sugar cane in Angola and in brigades studying the phytosanitary defense of tropical products in Portugal. He also wrote several reports in role as technical advisor at the Ministry of Economy (Rural) of Guinea-Conakry.

But while agronomists, geographers, and other specialists (even politically hostile ones) retain only observations of a purely scientific nature from objective inquiry, Cabral provided a penetrating *interpretation* of rural communities. This is explained by the fact that his knowledge and observation were illuminated by a conceptual device:

historical materialism. For him, it was not just about recording such things as agricultural production in colonial Portuguese Guinea. Instead, he deepened his analysis of socioeconomic structures, identified the stages of social and cultural development, deconstructed the mechanisms of exploitation—in short, he got to know the historical reality of his people.

However, it is important to bear in mind the conditions under which Amílcar Cabral's studies of agriculture and the rural economy were undertaken and published. The organization and execution of the 1953 agricultural census and subsequent scientific publications represent only the official side of his activities as an agricultural engineer and researcher—he was openly part of the colonial administration and press. This served as legal cover for his political activities. For this reason, one should not look for a finished expression of all of Cabral's observations and ideas about Guinean society in anything that he wrote at the time. Certainly, his duties as a technician, especially during the agricultural census, allowed him to make an in-depth study of the Guinean peasantry, their living conditions, their social organization, and their level of consciousness. He was also able to analyze the production system, the division of labor, and the instruments and techniques developed by Guinea's various ethnicities to show, without ambiguity, that the colonial system was culpable for the state of Guinean agriculture—whether it is the insufficient standard of living of African peasants, or the rapid soil degradation caused by export crops. Through this, he was able to denounce the shortcomings and neglect of the technical services of the colonial administration. One could even add that a large part of his revolutionary practice in the following years was based on intimate knowledge of the country's populations acquired during the 1953 agricultural census. However, Cabral only used a tiny part of this experience in his publications. Despite this, his works—and it's important to highlight this—distinguish themselves in relation to the specialized literature of the time, even within the official framework: his articles contained denunciations of racist and colonialist ideology; they showed how the technical problems of Guinean agriculture were linked to the colonial system and why any development program must necessarily be preceded by a transformation of African structures and the dominant social relations.

From his main terrain of experience, Cabral extended his field of reflection to the whole of black Africa. In one of his numerous articles, he explained the factors that condition the use of land, the agro-climatic complex, the essential characteristics of agriculture, the agrarian structure, and the crop systems, before analyzing, interpreting, and drawing conclusions about the "shifting cultivation" system:[71]

> The "shifting cultivation" system, despite providing, as has been said, a rational solution to the problem of agriculture in Black Africa, is reprehensible. This is fundamentally because it does not serve the progressive development of man. Does this mean that the pure and simple elimination of the shifting cultivation system is necessary?
>
> It must be admitted that, if new factors do not disturb the life of the black African, the evolution of agriculture would lead to the transformation of the system.
>
> In fact, this is what happens, as mentioned, in many regions of Black Africa. Transformation, rather than pure and simple elimination. Relative and not absolute negation. In other words: the evolution of African cultural techniques in order to better serve the progress of black African people cannot ignore the fact that they reflect a deep knowledge of the environment and its possibilities. The creation of new techniques is a necessity. But in order for such new techniques to be successful, they must take advantage of everything positive that the experience of centuries and reason has created.
>
> The fact that this vital need has not been met has resulted in true catastrophes. In general, at the base of these lies is the complex of factors introduced into the life of the black African by a new entity—colonialism.

When addressing the relationship between colonialism and the shifting cultivation system, Cabral points to the constraining economic factors which led Africans to change their mode of production, without altering the system of cultivating the land. He wrote:

> In short, colonialism introduces a new production system in Africa, translated into an *"économie de traite"* (a trade economy). However, it has kept the shifting cultivation system. Without taking into account the difference in mesological conditions, it applies, or tries to apply, European agricultural techniques to the shifting cultivation system because it is convinced of the "superiority" of these practices. The contradictions created mean that, day by day, the devastation of African land increases. All of the inconveniences prudently avoided by black African agriculture begin to appear. The example of Senegal has given us the term "senegalization" to describe the devastation of soil in Africa. The black man, powerless, watches or participates in his own destruction. With his life out of balance, having to satisfy not only new needs that have been created but also the demands of his new social condition, he gradually uproots himself, emigrates or is forced to emigrate, abandons or lacks the time to assimilate the wisdom that he himself, based on empirical knowledge of the environment and the experience of centuries, has created.

Cabral states that the direction of the evolution of agriculture in black Africa must take into account a series of needs:

a) take full advantage of all the resources of Black* Africa, which will require, in some aspects, the progressive transformation of nature;
b) apply the wealth from these resources to Africa itself;
c) establish an agrarian structure that does not allow the disorderly and greedy exploitation of the land; that does not allow exploitation, tout court, of man by man;
d) provide black men with access to all means of defense against climate adversity;

---

* In Andrade's citation of Cabral here and elsewhere, "Black" is capitalized when referring to Africa as a geopolitical reality. When in reference to black as a descriptor of people or a culture, the lowercase is used.

e) foster the cultural development of black Africans, which requires them to make the most of their own culture and those of other peoples;

f) select and take advantage of everything that is useful in black African land cultivation systems, as well as everything that is applicable to Black Africa from European techniques.

At the same time, as he was conducting the census, Cabral addressed other issues: for example, the mechanization of agriculture. This would be doomed to failure if appropriate solutions were not found to the complex problems of a technical and socioeconomic nature inherent to it: the identification in the tropical environment both of soils capable of being mechanized without harming fertility and soil defense on the one hand; and of the set of issues related to the situation of indigenous agricultural workers in the economic, social, and cultural context of Guinea-Bissau on the other.

Above all, Cabral emphasized the fundamental economic place occupied by African peasants in the economy of Guinea-Bissau. He established a distinction between the two styles of agricultural exploitation present in the country: that of *indigenous land* (the land that belongs to the community) and that of the *non-indigenous land* (the land belongs to an individual or collective entity that occupies it under a concession or freehold regime). The first is devoted to self-consumption and export products—almost exclusively groundnuts (*arachis hypogeae*) that are sold to foreign traders—while the second is mainly dedicated to the cultivation of sugar cane to manufacture brandy sold to indigenous people. The surveys carried out by Cabral demonstrate that rice is the most profitable crop for indigenous agriculture, while the groundnut is the one that causes the most damage. The price at which the peasant must sell his harvest in the store represents a derisory remuneration for the family work necessary for cultivation of the cash crop (groundnuts): most of the time only the minimum required to pay the tax. This is why the colonial administration had to employ force to ensure people would grow groundnuts. The identification of the features of economic exploitation for the immense majority of the Guinean population shows the direction of Amílcar Cabral's thoughts and actions: towards awareness of the peasant masses around their tangible objective interests and, in the first place, opposition to forced agriculture and the obligation to pay the hut tax. Among the conditions necessary for the progress of Guinean agriculture, he regards as most important "the establishment of agrarian structures compatible with the progressive development of populations, based on local traditions," i.e., on a collective basis, which means that any economic progress will depend on a political transformation of the dominant social system—nothing less than a revolution.[72]

II. An Outline of the Theory of the Struggle against Portuguese Colonialism

Since their foundation in 1956, the PAIGC and the MPLA contained undeniable similarities regarding the conception of nationalist unity and the role played by the *núcleo principal* [principal nucleus]. Marxist ideas penetrated the restricted circles of the African intelligentsia in Angola and Guinea-Bissau. A theoretically elaborated political text, opening up perspectives for the struggle in Guinea-Bissau and Cape Verde that did not exist at that time, unlike in Angola where the MPLA manifesto (written in December of that year) had already set out a project for a progressive society through the establishment of a "democratic and popular government." The first document outlines the overall international relationship of forces, characterizes the world-wide front against imperialism, describes the most glaring aspects of Portuguese colonialist oppression, and defines the enemy of the Angolan people. Also called for was the means to achieve liberation: a revolutionary struggle, whose triumph will be based on the constitution of "a united front of all anti-imperialist forces in Angola, regardless of political opinion, the social situation of individuals. Therefore, through the broadest popular movement for the liberation of Angola."

Thanks to his presence in the Angolan field of struggle, and his participation as an active participant in the emergence of the MPLA, Cabral contributed greatly by exposing the masses—and in particular the youth—to these key ideas.

The year 1957 saw the birth of his first draft of political analysis, which not only considered the strategy for the struggle against Portuguese colonial domination globally, but also regionally. In the light of the historical and concrete experience of the armed struggle, the minutes of the Consultation and Study Meeting for the Development of the Struggle Against Portuguese Colonialism[73] enable us to measure the pressures of ideological mimicry and dogmatism, as well as the failures to understand the social components of the colonized masses.

During the session on November 16, Amílcar Cabral explained the situation in Guinea and the Cape Verde islands.[74]

In his opinion, the following groups existed in Guinea and, due to the economic characteristics that define them, they should be included in the corresponding classes:

- the peasantry, made up of indigenous farmers who exploit the land as collective property;
- the proletariat, made up of workers in urban areas, commercial employees, workers in agricultural or rural companies, and civil servants (mostly occupying subordinate positions);
- craftsmen, which were disappearing and becoming proletarianized;
- the petite bourgeoisie, made up of rural landowners, urban landowners, and small traders;
- the bourgeoisie, represented by the owners of large monopoly companies.

The ethnic and regional distribution was described as follows:

1) in the peasantry, 90 percent of the population dedicated exclusively to agriculture and livestock was made up of blacks;
2) workers in urban areas were almost entirely black, with a tendency towards an increase in the number of whites;
3) commercial employees, made up of whites and blacks, with a tendency similar to the previous one;
4) civil servants, made up of whites and blacks (Cape Verdeans and those originally from São Tomé), with a tendency towards an increase in the number of Cape Verdeans and whites;
5) craftsmen, made up of rural landowning Cape Verdeans and Guineans;

6) most of them Cape Verdeans, who were engaged in horticulture, sugar cane, and rice cultivation);

7) urban property owners: in real estate, the number of Europeans tended to increase;

8) traders, those who had an established business: Europeans in the vast majority, but also Cape Verdeans and a minority of Guineans;

9) foreign monopolies: the CUF (Companhia União Fabril), which operated wholesale and retail trade, industry (rice, groundnuts, cashews), transport; Ultramarina, owner of Sociedade de Sabões; and BNU (Banco Nacional Ultramarino).

According to Cabral, workers in urban centers, or "proletarians," are those who created ties between the different zones or branches of production and therefore had a concrete vision of national unity. Commercial employees and civil servants, considered equally proletarian, were influenced by the mentality of colonialists and explorers.

Cabral addressed the issue of the social lever of the struggle and stated:

> The Guinean proletariat has the role of leading the anti-colonial struggle. There are great possibilities for achieving the necessary alliance between the proletariat and the peasantry. The petty bourgeoisie will be able to play the role of a revolutionary national bourgeoisie. Urban workers have the necessary conditions so that the work of raising political awareness can be immediately carried out among them, to the extent that they have a concrete vision of national unity.[75]

Despite its particular historical conditions, Cape Verde was a colony and the Cape Verdean people suffered two forms of oppression: oppression coming from the relations established between Portugal and the islands, and economic and social oppression by landowners, industrial traders, and other members of the bourgeoisie. Due to periodic drought and abandonment caused by poor management, a large number of rural properties had passed from Cape Verdean ownership to credit organizations (savings accounts and banks). Emigration is a product of poverty. Cabral did not draw a conclusion regarding the meaning of the demands of the Cape Verdean people that were directed simultaneously against colonial domination and internal economic and social oppression. According to his criteria, it was urgent to "encourage the organization of struggles that eliminate the conditions of oppression of the Cape Verdean people and place them among other peoples fighting against colonialism."

This entire, rather schematic, description of the socioeconomic structure in Guinea and Cape Verde, analogous in terms of methodology for other countries (São Tomé and Príncipe, Angola, Mozambique), guided the formulation of a principle defined by the participants at the meeting:

> The workers of the Portuguese colonies in Africa constitute the most revolutionary social class. The proletariat has the role of mobilizing and organizing the masses to lead the struggle against colonialism.

However, moving forward in time, not only did they regard the unity of the peoples and organizations of the Portuguese colonies as *indispensable* for the success of the struggle, but they were also committed to "accomplishing their liberation, united with the other African peoples" with a view to "the total liquidation of the imperialist yoke in Africa." Nationalist leaders correctly observed the physiognomy of the exploited strata—fruit of their own observation. But the bookish influence of ideological mimicry was so strong that they had not yet acquired the independence of spirit to identify the motive social forces of the liberation struggle on the basis of African realities. The theoretical reinterpretation of Marxism developed in the following years progressively rectified the dogmatic positions assumed at the Consultation and Study Meeting for the Development of the Struggle Against Portuguese Colonialism.

FIVE

The Decisive Turning Point

I. Theory and Practice. The First Confrontation: The Pidjiguiti Massacre

We have seen what constituted the theoretical basis for the Party's emphasis on such mass actions as strikes, wage demands, and petitions, these being a form of struggle centered on the vanguard of the working classes: the "proletariat" of the public squares, particularly in Bissau.

Workers at the Bissau port had already gained some experience of striking, which they had successfully done in February 1956.

Three years later, faced with an increasing cost of living, sailors on Casa Gouveia boats demanded a salary increase.[76] Not having achieved their aims, they prepared to begin another strike initially scheduled for July 31. They demonstrated a qualitatively superior level of organization and discipline: for two days, the individual and collective approach gave rise to solidarity from other categories of workers and found a favorable echo throughout the country. On August 3, 1959, faced with the refusal of the Gouveia bosses, the sailors, crews, and stevedores of all the river transport boats that used the Pidjiguiti pier decided to stop work.

These new *internal* factors awakened the vigilance of the repressive forces (PIDE [International and State Defense Police] was already active in Guinea-Bissau), who were aware of the clandestine existence of the party, the structure, and its organization and knew that "a part of the militants and even those responsible were made up of salaried workers, such as dockers and sailors." The *external* factor of the immediate African context—the proclamation of the independence

of the Republic of Guinea (the former French colony of Guinea)—
further reinforced the determination on the part of the colonial
administration to drown this attempt of rebellion at birth, given that
it was the "first organized manifestation of the political consciousness
of the working masses, in particular the workers of Bissau."

Amílcar Cabral viewed the event as evidence of the emergence
"of a new consciousness, which, in the current African and international context, could not but be the first vigorous manifestation of
our national, albeit embryonic, consciousness and the courageous
expression of our people to free themselves from colonial domination
as the other peoples of Africa were doing. And this manifestation of
awareness and determination to struggle was all the more significant
as the strike affected one of the main branches, if not the main branch,
of the colonial exploitation economy: the port and river transport, the
flow and the export of the riches of our land and of the fruits of the
labor of our people."[77]

The Pidjiguiti pier massacre,[78] perpetrated on August 3, 1959, left
more than fifty victims and hundreds injured, not to mention the
abuse and torture of people suspected of having a connection with
the party. Therefore, the date of August 3, 1959 has been symbolically
elevated to "the day of our African homeland."[79]

II. The Strategy of the PAIGC

The news of the Pidjiguiti massacre reached Amílcar Cabral during
his last trip to Angola, where he was supposed to carry out an important mission for the MPLA.[80] Returning to Bissau, he presided over a
meeting on September 19, 1959, three years after the founding of the
party, a meeting that would radically change the face of the struggle
against Portuguese colonial domination. PAIGC activists reviewed
the experience of years of clandestine political combat and analyzed
the situation of the country. It seemed clear to them that demonstrations and demands in urban centers, a strong zone of colonialism,
were not only ineffective, but also constituted an easy pretext for
repressive action by colonial forces. In light of the events in Pidjiguiti,
the nationalists noted that, due to the very nature of Portuguese colonialism, armed struggle was the only path likely to lead to national
liberation. Cabral explained:

Because we saw that against the Portuguese colonialists, as indeed against imperialism in general, there is no question of knowing whether to carry out an armed struggle or not, as it is always an armed struggle. Because the enemy always has weapons in his hand. Either he's the only one who has the weapons and we don't, or we're not crazy and we arrange to shoot them too. This is the truth of the struggle against imperialism, particularly against Portuguese colonialism, as they showed us on Pidjiguiti pier.[81]

With a view to moving to that new phase and adopting the principle of "expecting the best, but preparing for the worst," the extended meeting decided on a six-point action plan that stipulated the urgent need to:

1) immediately mobilize and organize the peasant masses, who have proven, through experience, to be the main physical force of the national liberation struggle;
2) strengthen the party organization in urban areas, but keep it clandestine, avoiding any and all public demonstrations;
3) develop and reinforce the unity of Africans from all ethnic groups, origins, and social strata around the Party;
4) prepare the largest possible number of cadres, both inside and outside the country, for the political direction of the organization and the victorious development of the struggle;
5) organize emigrants residing in neighboring countries in order to serve the liberation struggle and the future reconstruction of the country;
6) struggle to obtain the essential means to continue the struggle.

It was decided to transfer the General Secretariat of the Party abroad, in order to guarantee the safety of its key leaders and facilitate the reinforcement of international actions.

This meeting, as Cabral said, "was decisive for everything that happened next for our struggle."

Thus, the center of gravity moved from the city to the countryside. He wrote:

> We then decided to mobilize the countryside. Many people think that to decide and do this we would have to apply the theories of Mao Zedong . . . but we didn't even know them yet. The needs of our land are what led us to this approach, our own mistakes had shown us the way.

In parallel with this priority task and to ensure its success, the PAIGC proceeded with the unification of patriotic forces both inside and outside of Guinea. The FLGCV (Front for the Liberation of Guinea-Bissau and Cape Verde) Charter written by a certain "Abel Djassi" [Cabral's *nom de guerre*], bears the date of the extended meeting held in Bissau.[82] The regrouping of émigré and refugee organizations established in the republics of Senegal and Guinea gave rise to the creation of the Liberation Movement of Guinea-Bissau and Cape Verde (MLGC) and the Dakar conference, from July 12 to 14, 1961.*

The Party retained all of the initiative for operations within the national space, because it represented the *internal front*. The outbreak of the armed struggle and the progressive commitment of the best cadres in the ranks of the PAIGC would render the continuity of political organizations established outside the country meaningless. The years of transition (1960–62) constituted one of the most fruitful periods, revealing the ability of the masses to adhere to new political ideas and the rooting of the Party. These years truly shaped the future of the liberation struggle. The mobilization of social strata, as we will examine later, is conducted at various levels and on different planes, following a strategy that takes into account all aspects of the situation, the internal and external factors.

But what did the PAIGC want?[83] According to a document dated July 14, 1960, it aimed to achieve two essential objectives: achieving national independence for the people of Guinea-Bissau and Cape Verde and building peace, progress, and happiness.[84]

---

* [In the original French, Andrade has an additional footnote on the MLGC which reads "*insert french italics*," or "That same year, after the independence of Guinea, small groups were created, which the party managed to bring together in a coherent way around itself. There was only one organization left [the PAIGC] and no one claimed to belong to any other group. This demonstrated the confidence people had in the party leadership."]

The statutes and general bases of the program would be defined a year later.

Expanding the scope of its strategy and following the example of the MPLA a few months earlier, the PAIGC sent a lengthy memorandum to the Portuguese government.[85] The memorandum, which placed the phenomenon of "decolonization" in its historical and general context, tried to convince Lisbon to decolonize quickly to protect its own interests. The PAIGC's preliminary condition was recognition of the right to self-determination enshrined in the United Nations Charter. PAIGC leaders appealed—without much conviction—for an intervention from most of the states represented at the UN to resolve the open conflict between the people of the colonies and the Portuguese government. In this sense, the PAIGC was proposing a framework for negotiation. But Portugal, under the thumb of its obsolete dictator, Salazar, a byproduct of fascism, found itself structurally unable to carry out any decolonization process. By mortgaging its colonial wealth in Angola and Mozambique, it gained the economic, financial, and military support that it needed to undertake a preventive war and, if the situation so developed, face an armed struggle. The PAIGC memorandum received the same short shrift given to its MPLA counterpart.[86]

Then came February 4, 1961, the date on which the Angolan people brutally broke the veil of Portuguese colonialism and erupted onto the stage of history. This accelerated Guinea's commitment to the same path. Once again, Amílcar Cabral addressed an open letter to the Portuguese government on October 13, 1961, which ended thus:

> If the Portuguese Government insists on not reconsidering its position—which disregards the interests of our people and is also contrary to those of the people of Portugal—no force will be able to prevent our Party from fulfilling its historic mission: that of developing our national liberation struggle, responding with violence to the violence of the Portuguese colonialist forces, and completely liquidating colonial domination in Guinea and Cape Verde by all possible means.[87]

The Portuguese government's reaction to the protest movement that was so widespread in its colonies could be summarized as follows:

announcements about institutional reforms with the intention of making all indigenous people civilized so that they could be turned into Portuguese.

In view of this "ferociously negative" position, as Cabral put it, the decision was made to proclaim direct action on August 3, 1961—"the day of the transition of our revolution from the phase of political struggle to that of national insurrection in the form of direct action against the Portuguese colonialists."[*]

The unifier of the Guinean and Cape Verdean peoples was now experiencing a political practice that went beyond the narrow borders of this territorial space. Cabral compared his experience with the facts on the ground in Africa. He put theoretical knowledge about revolutionary changes in the world to the service of a rigorous understanding of specific realities of the peoples of the Portuguese colonies. With this perspective, Cabral actively participated in the drafting of a collective document known as the MAC (Anti-Colonial Movement) Manifesto.[88]

The MAC Manifesto, which had already moved beyond refuting fallacious arguments and denouncing the crimes of colonialism, clarified the positions of the nationalist movements vis-à-vis fundamental problems and indicated the paths to follow and the means to employ in the struggle for national independence. It regarded "raising, developing, and coordinating the unity of Africans in the struggle against Portuguese colonialism" as essential. Its stated objective was "the immediate conquest of national independence and the total liquidation of Portuguese colonialism." It refuted the thesis that the inhabitants of the colonies were too "immature for self-determination," which was still widespread among Portuguese progressive organizations, and argued that "in no case could oppression constitute a school of virtues and skills for any people." Taking the view that "Salazarism" is not the main enemy, the Manifesto stated that freedom and progress in colonized countries could not be dependent on a political-social revolution in Portugal. The document proclaimed the right of the people to make their own decisions, this being the only basis on which they were ready to collaborate with the Portuguese people.

After making the historical observation that colonial wars are no longer conducted within the framework of the absolute supremacy

---

[*]   For the full text of the proclamation, see: *Unity & Struggle*, Monthly Review Press, 1979, p. 174.

of the worldwide imperialist front, the Manifesto then spoke in favor of the peaceful liquidation of colonialism, at the same time as it denounced the Portuguese government and held it responsible for the armed conflicts that it was preparing to unleash. Finally, the Manifesto discussed the wide range of aspects, forms, and means of the liberation struggle: "Our struggle must profoundly negate and destroy colonialism. This movement will create the future conditions for life in freedom."

Where violence is resorted to in order to destroy the structure and forces of colonialism, how should it be done? The outline of an answer to this fundamental question is the following: sabotage, paralysis, and destruction, i.e., unleashing the most appropriate forms of armed struggle against Portuguese colonialism in a just war of national liberation.[89]

Knowing and making known the enemy's designs in order to better combat it should be carried out among the militants directly involved and also among African and international opinion, which remained poorly informed and was frequently deceived by Portuguese colonial ideology. Cabral's English-language pamphlet and the first report he presented to the UN special committee were part of the strategy of internationally isolating the Portuguese colonialists.[90] The fundamental traits of the political thought that Cabral would go on to deepen throughout his life as a leader were defined as early as 1961. In the concert of triumphant speeches of circumstance, he recalled the need to examine the core of the events which characterized the so-called Year of Africa (1960): to discover the causes, nature, and effects of the various failures and errors. The tragic physical elimination of Congolese president Patrice Lumumba being the most revelatory.

For the first time, Cabral defined the purpose of the African revolution and the means of achieving it:

> For us, the African revolution means transforming the current economic life of African societies towards progress. A precondition for this transformation is the elimination of foreign economic domination.[91]

The historical stage that the continent was going through was understood as follows: it was urgent to overcome the phase of the "conquest of political autonomy, despite the persistence of classical colonialism in some areas" to concentrate efforts on the struggle against neocolonialism. Cabral goes further and finally affirms the existence of a crisis in the African revolution, the nature of which arises from a crisis of knowledge, in other words, from the insufficiency, if not the lack, of theoretical bases for the concrete analysis of concrete situations. According to him, in order to be able to act in accordance with the possible conditions of the moment, it would be necessary to satisfy three conditions:

a) concrete knowledge of the reality of each country and of Africa, as well as the experiences of other peoples;
b) the preparation, on a scientific basis, of the principles that should guide the march of our people towards progress (the liberation struggle and economic reconstruction);
c) the definition of practical measures to be adopted in each particular case.

The two documents presented at the conference of the nationalist organizations of Guinea and Cape Verde (which took place in Dakar, July 1961), that is, the speech by the PAIGC delegation, on the one hand, and the general report, on the other hand, developed the ideas set out in the speech. The speech traced the evolution of the PAIGC, the stages already passed, and defined the tasks of preparation for the final phase of the liberation struggle.

It also outlined the contours of the progressive society to be built in Guinea and Cape Verde in line with the PAIGC Major Program.[92] In the general report, which occupies an important place in his ideological itinerary, Amílcar Cabral carried out a broader examination of the essential characteristics of the time and stated that:

> More than the class struggle in capitalist countries and the antagonism between these countries and the socialist world, the liberation struggle of colonial peoples is the essential characteristic, we would even say the principal motor of the advancement of history in our time; our national liberation struggle against Portuguese colonial-

ism is an integral part of this struggle, of this conflict, which is taking place on three continents.[93]

Cabral returned to a key idea of the MAC Manifesto: the liquidation of colonialism would engender the liquidation of fascism in Portugal. He clarified both the meaning of the action to be developed to resolve the main contradiction (which opposed "the interests of our people and those of the Portuguese colonialists") and the content of African unity and international solidarity. Cabral would go on to make effective use of the weapons of critique to dominate the new situation that was approaching: the people's war.

Part III.
Sociology of People's War*

---

*   The first two chapters that follow were taken, with slight changes, from a communication by the author at the Twenty-Fourth International Congress of Sociology held in Algiers, in March 1974. See: *The People's War in Guinea-Bissau. Cadernos livres* n. 1. Edições Sá da Costa [Andrade], 1974.

SIX

The People's War:
A Model or a Path?

Among Third World revolutionary experiences, that of Vietnam most closely resembles the case of a certain African country in an armed struggle for its complete national liberation—Guinea-Bissau. Certain characteristics of Vietnamese society, its former colonial situation, the ideology that guides the struggle of its people, and finally the historical consequences in terms of the relationship between international forces that its victories gave rise to, naturally meant that theory and practice of the Việt Minh constituted the principal source of inspiration for Guinea-Bissau's revolutionary project.

In a famous text, General Giáp clearly defined the stages of development and the principles of the war of the Vietnamese people.[94] Thus, the *decisive* matter was to educate, mobilize, organize, and arm all the people so that they participated in the resistance. The fundamental issue, from a political point of view, was the unity of the people, the mobilization of all energies for resistance, and the National Front united against the imperialists and their lackeys. Its *essence* was a national democratic revolution conducted in armed form, whose fundamental task was the overthrow of imperialism and the feudal landowner class, the former being the priority. The factors of success were that it be a just war which had a revolutionary armed force, a broad and solid united National Front, and a people power established at the time of the August Revolution which was, above all, organized and directed by the party of the working class: the Indochinese Communist Party.

In short, the political objectives of this resistance consisted of radically resolving the two fundamental contradictions of Vietnamese
society—the main contradiction between the nation and imperialism,
on the one hand, and, on the other, the contradiction between the
people (especially the peasants) and the feudal property-owning class—
in opening the path to socialism for the Vietnamese Revolution.

General Giáp highlighted a general principle:

> The sacred resistance of our people, which continued the
> great work of the August Revolution, eloquently proved
> that, in the current world situation, a nation, however small
> and weak, that has risen as if it were one man under the
> leadership of the working class to struggle resolutely for
> its independence and democracy is, in fact, morally and
> materially capable of defeating all aggressors, whatever they
> may be. Under certain historical conditions, this struggle
> for national liberation may, in order to achieve success, go
> through a long armed struggle—long-term resistance.

However, he added another tonality to this principle by stating:

> The revolutionary armed struggle is subject, in any
> country, to general fundamental laws. But it also involves,
> in each country, its own particularities and laws.[95]

Which means that to achieve universality, our knowledge capital must
be fed by specific data. The conditions of space and time provide cor-
rectives to tactics and even strategy.

The conception of the struggle of the Vietnamese people was based
on class dialectics, on the point of convergence between national consciousness and class consciousness. The very notion of "people" was
clarified from a class point of view, Vietnamese historian Nguyễn
Khắc Viện recalls:

> The people are everyone, rich and poor, Buddhists and Con-
> fucians, Catholics and atheists, majority and minority eth-
> nicities; but it is first of all the workers and poor peasants.[96]

Distinguishing the motive forces of the revolution from the forces that direct it, and the forms of action that the revolutionary movement can take from the fundamental ideas that guide it, Nguyễn concludes on the subject of the peasant essence of his country's revolution that:

> Those who claim that the Vietnamese revolution is a peasant revolution see only one stage of this revolution, that of armed struggle, with rural bases. They don't see that these bases were created by activists coming from the city, workers, and intellectuals. It was not the peasants who exerted their influence over these city men; it was city dwellers who shaped peasant organizations with ideas born in the city and formed new peasants in their image. [...] They only became revolutionary to the extent that they adopted the ideology of the working class.[97]

In short, the historical experience of the Việt Minh rested on the sociological cohesion of the people, a national factor acquired millennia ago, on what from a socioeconomic point of view was a colonial situation, but in which there was a profound differentiation of classes, and around the ideology of the working class.

Furthermore, the Vietnamese communists realized, according to Jean Chesnay's formulation, "the equation between revolutionary movement and national movement."

During the preliminary phase of the national liberation movement in the Portuguese colonies, the exemplary character of the Vietnamese resistance, the heroic greatness of its human dimension, the global reach of its triumph imposed themselves before our eyes as the *model* of the revolutionary project that we proposed to carry out in our countries. This is how our first analyses of the *anatomy* of our societies sought at all costs the social component (the working class) that bears history. This attempt translated into a mobilization of what was then inappropriately called the proletariat of the cities. This did not stand the test of facts.

We have therefore learned, to our cost, that there is no *single*, preestablished model for the liberation struggle and that the ascension to the universality of laws passes through the appropriation of concrete, specific situations—the démarche of thought that defines the *national* path of the people's war. This is not, in any way, to diminish, or even less reject, the ideology of the working class and its universal value, or to circumscribe it to one geo-sociological space. The aim is, very modestly, to enrich it with new data and bronze it beneath the comrade "sun of Africa."

SEVEN

Emergence of the People's War

The alienating and subjugating historical conditions of classical colonialism triggered the people's war in Africa, and particularly in Guinea-Bissau. To be absolutely precise, we are talking about the most anachronistic and most retrograde classical colonialism, guided by an ideology of domination explained concretely in a *primitive racism*:[98] Portuguese colonialism.

Guinea-Bissau, until the first military actions, presented the most pronounced characteristic features of a colony framed by exploitation. From the point of view of economic dominance, it constituted, together with the islands of Cape Verde and São Tomé and Príncipe, the truly Portuguese territorial subset. While in Angola and Mozambique the capital that was accumulated was essentially of non-Portuguese origin, in Guinea-Bissau things happened differently. In Guinea-Bissau, the import and export of capital took place in an exclusively Portuguese cycle. Furthermore, the real contact between the people of Guinea and the Portuguese was made through the traditional chiefs, the *sipaios*, and the *assimilados* who were assigned the roles of assistants in the administrative machine. It was, therefore, a colony based on commercial exports, the hut tax, and forced labor. Within this framework, so-called indigenous agriculture was intended entirely for the exchange economy. The land was not in external ownership. This social universe contained its own internal contradictions.

The peasants (a social layer and by no means a class), the Balantas, and other related groups—those without a state—did not present a class stratification, whereas groups such as the Fulas, the Mandingas, and the Manjacos already had ruling classes. Between these ruling classes and the others lay the main internal contradiction. Since the countryside was the essential element of the Guinean economy, this contradiction was more important than the contradiction in the cities between African bosses and the mass of subordinate employees. Considered from a historical point of view and in relation to society in general, the layer of poor peasants, who were doubly exploited (both in commercial exchange with the Portuguese and in the work provided to their traditional chiefs), came to constitute the main physical strength of the national liberation struggle, but not the most important one.

In colonial society and the type of economic exploitation engendered by it, the role of the peasantry was fundamental.

Cabral explained:

> It can be said that everyone belongs to the peasantry, because everyone lives thanks to the products of the land. Even employees who earn their salaries live off groundnuts, palm oil, etc., as there is no industry in our country. All of Guinea's income comes from the land.[99]

The peasant layer should therefore be *vitally* interested in the struggle for social change, given that *objective* conditions have induced it to do so. However, it lacked *subjective* determination in the sense of awareness of the exploitation carried out indirectly through trade, due to the difference between products' prices and their value. This class consciousness came from abroad. It was not, therefore, within the peasantry that the social fraction capable of playing a driving role in triggering the national liberation struggle and taking on the demands of other exploited layers could be found. In the urban environment, the driving forces came together: sectors of civil servants, commercial employees, small, *déclassé* agricultural landowners, and the revolutionary petite bourgeoisie. The strongest social layer, the most *important* from a historical point of view, was made up of wage earners and the petite bourgeoisie. The petite bourgeoisie became the antagonistic *vector* of political and sociocultural change in the solution to the global contradiction by opposing the entire people to foreign oppression.

The outbreak of the people's war in Guinea made it necessary to carry out a concrete analysis of the concrete situation in the country—this is glaringly evident today. In Cabral's understanding, this was all about understanding the historical, ethnic, geographic, economic, social, and cultural reality—all supported by the most important reality in terms of struggle: the political reality. The people's war was part of the dialectical game of positive and negative aspects, of strengths and weaknesses, that this political reality entails.

The absence of mountains, the extreme economic underdevelopment, the social calamities and the misery that weighed on *thingified* populations, the obscurantism and cultural backwardness, the crushing and fragmentation of ethnicities resulting from historical facts and the division maintained by the enemy—all these weaknesses together were insufficient to block the process of unleashing the armed struggle for national liberation. These fundamental particularities of colonial Guinea were reciprocally opposed to those of Portugal: a weak European power, aided by its allies from the imperialist camp, that was determined to defend the colonial system in order to have the resources (in terms of personnel and materials) to maintain itself. The political and social character of the regime, which was fascist in nature, reduced, if not eliminated, the possibility of a popular uprising against the eventuality of a colonial war of aggression. Appraised from the perspective of the development of the confrontation which was to follow, its human, military, financial, and material resources would eventually be exhausted, and the retrograde nature of the war would lead Portugal into isolation.

But how could it be *possible* to accomplish what in the eyes of the masses seemed to be *impossible*? Through the creation of a party to act as the vanguard of the people—an instrument capable of leading the masses to understand the nature of their own exploitation, then of mobilizing them, giving them a framework, a political consciousness so that they would support the war, of transforming them into militants, and of founding the nation. A party, the PAIGC, guided by a revolutionary theory.

Returning to the profile that distinguishes the Vietnamese reality from the Guinean reality given their respective social components and their leading political force: in Vietnam, the workers and poor peasants clearly constituted the central core of the people under the leadership of the Indochinese Communist Party. But in Guinea, notions of "the people" encompassed a wider grouping of all those who supported the armed struggle against Portuguese colonialism and collaborated openly or clandestinely with the Party.[100] The PAIGC presented itself with the rigorous characteristics of a national liberation movement at the forefront of the struggle for independence.

EIGHT

Viability of the Sociology of War

If sociology aims to "study social laws in different areas of action and covering more or less simple social phenomena,"[101] this process naturally requires scientific knowledge.

In its motivations as well as throughout its development, the national liberation struggle—and, according to Cabral, this can only be fully accomplished through a revolution—calls for increasingly larger sectors, fractions, layers, or classes of the whole social structure to participate. The struggle summons, gathers, and concentrates the engines of change around the party, the movement, or the front, as it reverses the strength of the dominant (colonial) society. The ordering of the social forces emerges from the first, numerically small, core of leaders, thus breaking with the old order in which they were inserted.

As for the particular case of the struggle in Guinea-Bissau, the stages of its development followed a scheme that comprised, firstly, mobilization and armed propaganda, followed by the organization of specific activity within social relations.

Faced with the new realities engendered by war, individuals, different social groups, and even ethnicities revealed and adopted behaviors whose explanation does not come mechanically from their social origins. This reality can also contribute to a better interpretation of certain attitudes.

We are taken by the sociological foundation of Amílcar Cabral's thought throughout the major phases of the struggle: the mobilization of social forces, the commitment to armed conflict, and the establishment of counterpower.

I. Mobilization and Its Language

Mobilization immediately translates into the search for an appropriate language, aimed at social groups that face the daily reality of
colonial exploitation. To grasp all the data in their full scope, it would
be necessary to examine the testimony of the social actors who took
on the mission of propagating the idea of armed struggle among the
peasants.[102] Cabral himself, on the threshold of 1960, ran the first
cadre school in Conakry. There, parallel to general political training,
he taught these cadres the arguments and language to use in order to
speak to the Guinean people colonized in the countryside. The social
origin of these young activists (coming from the fringes of the wage
earners, the petite bourgeoisie, and the *lumpenproletariat*, floating
between urban centers and the countryside) indicates their status as
intermediate cadres, indispensable in this decisive phase. The Secretary General of the PAIGC* possessed exceptional qualities. Enlight-
ened by in-depth knowledge of the mentality of the peasant farmers,
encouraged by their insight and creative initiative, he introduced a
verbal methodology in terms of what should be said to men immersed
in colonial darkness. These first shadow activists would become the
illuminators of the path to national independence.

Let us quickly examine the content and political purpose of the
pamphlets written in the alert and precise style of "Abel Djassi."[103]
These messages, addressed to representatives of different social strata,
contain part of the sociology of motivation toward armed struggle.
Since they dealt with leading an entire people to commit themselves
to combat, and on a *national* basis, no socio-professional category or
social group could be excluded.

Cabral appealed to public servants and commercial employees, all
kinds of workers, traditional chiefs, soldiers forcibly recruited into the
colonial army—a representative range of colonized society—to become
aware of the situation of concrete exploitation in which they lived,
with the perspective of a commitment that would change their destiny.

He employed *slogans* adapted to the imminent *historical moment*: to
associate the life of each element of the population, whatever their role in
the hierarchy of colonial dependence, with that of the masses who are the

---

*   Cabral

workers of history, so that each post could be transformed into a fortress in the battle for the immediate destruction of Portuguese colonialism.

This was all toward raising the consciousness of the nature of exploitation and overcoming individual revolt to take on political commitment. Through the pamphlets, everyone found themselves placed in front of a mirror that reflected the image of the system's domination: social and racial discrimination, forced complicity in colonial domination, and the foreclosure of promotion and professional mobility. Cabral made these subalterns, located on the lowest administrative scale, understand that the uncertainty of tomorrow will be resolved through the confidence that characterizes the liberating struggle. Whatever (miserly) material privileges that one or another social category may have benefitted from within the framework of the colonial system, these privileges had to be placed in parallel with the *determining* factor: the attitude to embrace the struggle. The time to make the *definitive* choice had come: either you were a patriot or a servant of colonialism. It was urgent to speak and act. In view of the urgent need for the total liquidation of colonialism, one directive was constant: clandestine organization, contact, and adherence to the political formations of the PAIGC and the FLGCV.

The texts reveal Cabral's deep understanding of the concrete situation in which Guineans lived. But the messages were also directed at the main agents of colonial power (represented by the military and settlers). Soldiers, sergeants, and officers were called upon to turn their arms against their fascist superiors. Guinea's character as a colony of trade and not of white settlement determined whether colonists would adopt a *hesitant* or an *indifferent* attitude to the armed struggle. Cabral wrote:

> We distinguish between Portuguese colonialism and Portuguese settlers, just as we distinguish between a car and its wheels.

> [...] If you do not have the courage to support our struggle, preserve your dignity as men by refusing to serve the Portuguese colonialists, and by remaining neutral in the face of our liberation struggle.[104]

II. Understanding the Behaviors of Combatants
in the Phase of Armed Engagement

In light of the PAIGC documents and official statements by the Portuguese authorities, the military situation in Guinea (particularly in
the south) at the end of 1963, at the end of the first year of military
actions, was *excellent* for the nationalists.

Who were the artisans of this success? It was the party's combatants "coming from the forests, swamps, and distant villages [. . .],
armed with efficient material, with courage and discipline, as well as
knowledge of the concrete conditions and objectives of our struggle
and, as always, with the unconditional support of our people."

Viewed from the operational angle of armed action, the behavior of
combatants is not, at this stage, the object of any criticism, at least apparently. The outside observer does not see the inner life of the guerrilla in
the communiqués and reports of 1963–64, nor does he penetrate his
true social nature. The entire universe of men's conduct remains hidden.

In effect, the Secretary General (Cabral) speaks of the consistent
application of the strategy defined by the party, the high level of
effectiveness achieved by the struggle, the vigor of the combat, and
the political awareness of the people, at the same time that he recom-
mends the need to *improve* every day on the dual plane of political and
military action. It is true that the Battle of Como constituted a *test*, by
allowing us to gain consciousness of our strength, capacity to resist,
and as a means of testing the correctness of strategy and fighting
tactics. But it also made clear political and military problems which
"unexpectedly revealed deficiencies and errors, some of which could
become dangerous for our Party and our struggle."

The awareness of these problems and their discussion took place
during the Cassacá Congress, held at the precise moment when hard
fighting was taking place on the island of Como:

> Subjecting the deficiencies and errors committed within
> the Party to severe criticism and sincere self-criticism, our
> Congress has determined the necessary measures to elim-
> inate these faults.[105]

Reading this text intended for foreign readers does not allow us to
understand, in itself, the true nature, the *essence* of the problems, defi-

ciencies, errors, or faults. It is therefore necessary to become familiar with other internal documents to understand the behavior of the militants in the face of the new issues raised by their insertion in the war, the attitudes of those responsible, the first manifestations of abusive use of power—in other words, of *misconduct*. In one of his conversations at the cadre seminar, when carrying out a historical retrospective of the struggle, Amílcar Cabral evoked this period of the *glorious* work of mobilization by comparing the current combatants with the exemplary image of the first militants—"courageous mobilizers, with pistol in hand [. . .], suffering deprivation, the trials of hunger, being held captive by the PIDE." He added:

> But as we grew up and things improved, people began to take a breath and rest a little. We heard them saying: The others can work; I'm not doing anything else. I'll find a way to get out of it as much as I can.[106]

At this point, Cabral concluded:

> It's a shame, because otherwise, our struggle would have already ended. If we had advanced with the same audacity as we did in the initial moments of our armed struggle—for example, when we attacked the Portuguese with only a few weapons—if today, with the weapons we have, cannons, mortars, bazookas, and our experience, if today the comrades decided the following: I will not rest for a day, I will attack the Portuguese every day, the war would already be over.[107]

Cabral clearly deplored the progressive loss of the spirit of initiative and audacity that was characteristic of the mobilization phase—those essential qualities that would have led to the rapid military defeat of enemy troops. The Party was sick after a year of armed struggle. The Congress of Cassacá[108] allowed the leadership to diagnose the *social body* and treat it urgently, in situ:

> In the liberated regions of the south (to the north, only Oio had been liberated), Quínara, Fulacunda, Cubisseco,

N'tuane, Tchon di Nalu, etc., the comrades did not understand each other: each one acted in their own way, committing abuses at will, lacking respect for anyone who
presented themselves as their hierarchical superior.[109]

Among the flaws and faults that were revealed and constituted the
main deviations from the Party's line of conduct were:

- militarism and "commandism," a marked tendency to
  privilege the instrumental aspect of armed action to
  the detriment of political reality while seeking blind
  obedience from combatants;
- *regulundade*, the spirit of a boss, around which a
  clientele forms;
- *catchorindade*, i.e., servility;
- *mandjoandade*[110] or "clan spirit," based on a transfer of
  the chain of solidarity traditionally linked to age.

Alongside militarism, other typical abuses of authority include polyg-
amy and *griotism*, whereby a chief is praised in song by a griot [a type
of West African troubadour known as a *djidiu* in Guinean Creole].
In Cabral's opinion, these abuses resulted from the contradiction
of mentalities between ancient superstructures and modern ideas.
Observance of the new laws and the entrenchment of the Party's
methods were accompanied by a certain degree of violence against the
weight of traditional structures. It was therefore necessary to instill
confidence in the people and show them what the Party wanted to say.

Cabral, who always attached great importance to the ethical aspect
of the responsibilities of militants, summarized the general teachings
of the Congress of Cassacá in these terms:

The greatest danger in our struggle is not the Portuguese
beating us, because we don't have to let them do it if we
don't want to. The biggest danger is that we let the struggle
pass us by, stifling ourselves, not moving forward with our
struggle, staying behind, in old habits, in good spirits, not
respecting or fulfilling the Party's slogans as we should.[111]

III. The Characterization and Means of Overcoming Misconduct After the Congress of Cassacá

According to Party documents and statements by its leaders, a *major phase* of the war began after the Cassacá Congress. The implementation of the decisions taken during the Congress, their constant adaptation and adjustment to the new stages of the situation, continued to be a point of reference for militant action.

Cabral continued the fight against all manifestations of opportunism, such as the *racism*, regarded as "opportunism of the worst kind":

> We cannot measure each person's patriotism or sincerity
> by the color of their skin, the name they have or the way
> they dress.

Cabral always explained misconduct in terms of social and economic constraints and cultural backwardness.

Cassacá produced a shock. Many questions were raised during the congress and a gap was revealed: there was no guiding document for the application of the Party's principles. Amílcar Cabral dedicated himself to this task, after having deeply studied the teachings of the Vietnamese resistance. *Palavras de ordem gerais,* addressed to combatants and militants and written in November 1965, was the first text to cover the theory and practice of guerrilla warfare.[112] Prior to its publication, Cabral had dismantled the mechanisms of colonial domination, had called on all social strata of the country to take up arms, and had established the guiding principles of mobilization and contact with the working masses, particularly the peasantry. In summary, he had established the victorious balance of the first years of the war. However, Cabral had not yet carried out a global reflection on the essence of the war, a special situation that "requires special behavior from everyone, particularly from the men and women who engage in it."

Palavras de ordem gerais is divided into eight chapters. It provides a clear exposition of political principles, a set of directives for social praxis, a critique of the misconduct of Party leaders and a frame of

---

* The section "General Watchwords" in *Unity & Struggle,* published by Monthly Review Press. A direct translation would be "General Words of Order."

reference to explain and resolve problems during the course of the war. Take cognizance of dynamic reality at every moment, extract lessons from mistakes and victories, *think to act and act to think better*—these are not mere impressive formulas for the needs of revolutionary rhetoric, but the expression of the dialectical unity of thought and action.

This intellectual démarche was of such great importance that in November 1966, Cabral wrote a document entitled *Para a reorganização das Forças Armadas Revolucionárias do Povo (FARP)* [For the Reorganization of the Revolutionary Armed Forces of the People], in which he established a sociological relationship between misconduct and the social origins of the combatants. He insisted that an understanding of war was of fundamental importance:

> We must pay the greatest attention, knowing as best we can the essential characteristics of each phase of our struggle. We have to know well what the enemy's situation is, to try to discover from his own actions and attitudes what his plans are, and to see clearly what his main difficulties, weaknesses, and strengths are.

This text first analyzes the enemy's situation, its strengths and weaknesses. It circumscribes the characterization of the enemy in these terms: "The Portuguese government and the ruling circles in Portugal and in our country, which represent the interests of capitalists and other rich classes in Portugal, as well as non-Portuguese capital (i.e., American, English, German, capital, etc.) that has interests in Portugal, in our country, and in other Portuguese colonies."

Cabral distinguishes different behaviors among the Portuguese people and their classes in relation to the colonial war. There are exploiters and victims. Likewise, within the armed forces, the material and social situations of the different components unquestionably dictated divergent positions: senior officers (especially career personnel) benefited from the war, while militia officers were its victims; career sergeants were not the same as militia sergeants; and finally, soldiers, normally from the lower classes (workers and peasants), in spite of hating military life, were being forced to wage war. This bundle of contradictions and conflicts of interests is increasingly amplified, "not only within the Portuguese people and the colonialist armed forces, but also among the leaders themselves and the ruling classes in Portugal, between the Lisbon government and the colonial government in our country, between it and the General Staff, between the officers within each command, and between officers and their troops in general."[113] All of this constituted an important *weakness* of the enemy.

As for the enemy's forces, these rested on external and internal factors.

External Factors

    a)   the support of its NATO allies;

    b)   the economic weakness of Portugal, an underdeveloped country—

an apparent paradox that deserves an explanation: Portugal did not have the economic conditions to *grant* independence and then promote the exploitation of its colonies, as practiced by the imperialist powers. This *intrinsic* need to completely dominate Guinea on a political and economic level is a strength of the enemy—

    c)   ignorance, backwardness, and the situation of political and social oppression in which the Portuguese people live; subjected as they are to fascist repression and colonialist propaganda—these people, who do not easily understand the nature of the national liberation struggle, had not proven capable of organizing a large mass movement against the colonial government;

    d)   the divisions and disagreements between African states; Independent Africa is not capable of making all the necessary efforts to help the Guinean people and all others who find themselves in a similar situation.

Internal Factors

    a)   the lack of material goods of great value or large investments belonging to the Portuguese in Guinea, which explains the destruction caused by [Portuguese] bombings;

b) the betrayal or indifference, in the face of the struggle, of most sectors of the petty bourgeoisie: the majority of African employees of the colonial state (administrators, secretaries, post chiefs, officers, interns, engineers, etc.), as well as commercial employees and individuals engaged in a liberal profession (doctors, lawyers, agricultural technicians) have adopted an attitude of betrayal or indifference;

c) the betrayal of some of the *leaders* generally appointed by the colonial power;

d) the lack of national consciousness of a large part of the people: the direct agents of colonial rule relied on old tribal conflicts and wars. In the cities, they sought to promote separation between *mestiços* and blacks, senior officials and small officials, the petty bourgeoisie of Cape Verdean origin and that of Guinean origin, between employees and workers, etc. In the bush, the idea that each ethnic group has its own land did not allow for the development of national consciousness. A national consciousness is being acquired through the current process of struggle;

e) the troops and weapons of the colonialists: the enemy still has ample (technological, material, human) capacity to wage war, despite the fact that the Portuguese troops have found themselves in a difficult position and their matériel has lost its operational power;[114]

f) the weaknesses, errors, and deficiencies of the struggle, in particular the Party.

[Cabral says] the enemy counts on our weaknesses as a safe and decisive ally. We can even say that, in the current phase of our struggle, only we ourselves can destroy our Party. Our weaknesses are therefore the enemy's main strength in the current phase of our struggle.

In dynamic terms, this was about focusing attention on the enemy's weaknesses and strengths.

The Enemy's Main Weaknesses

a) our current great capacity to confront colonialist troops, our human and material forces, our growing capacity to destroy their living and material forces;

b) the divisions within the Portuguese people and in particular within the colonialist troops who are waging an unjust war in our land;

c) the fact that a major part of the colonialist troops did not know our land and our people and had to wage war in a different and, in some respects, a hostile environment.

Its Main Strengths

a) its troops and material, i.e., its urban barracks, its planes, and its boats;

b) the traitorous Africans who serve the colonialists;

c) the weaknesses, errors, and deficiencies of our Party, namely anything that could divide us or take away the support of the people.

Cabral focuses on characterizing the situation seen from an internal point of view and the development of the struggle. Starting from nothing, profound changes have already taken place in the lives of the people. A new man is being forged—the new social being—the greatest victory of the liberation struggle and the Party.

The most important political factor in the liberated regions is the increasingly broad participation of the population in the direction of our lives through the Party's base committees and other governing bodies. Our people are, for the first time, having the experience of being masters of their own destiny in the daily school of a revolutionary democracy in full development.

He attributes the errors and deficiencies in the armed struggle to the failure to fully apply the Party's slogans:

- a tendency towards improvisation;
- a lack of planning;
- failure to take into account the factor of time;
- lack of serious study on the part of leaders, added to improvisation, resulting in a lack of effective coordination of military forces;
- insufficient performance in terms of the courage of the combatants and the weapons used;
- indiscipline and abuse of authority;
- disagreements between some leaders;
- abuses in relations between the armed forces and the people.

Certain acts of hostility limited to some regions are more the result of mistakes made than a lack of patriotism on the part of the populations.

On the political level, Cabral highlights the tendency towards the monopolization of power: the right to command. He notes a certain passive resistance in the practical application of the Party's slogans, especially in relation to the integration of women and the nonobservance of fundamental principles regarding democratic centralism, criticism, self-criticism, and revolutionary democracy.

He also addressed the *moral plane,* which he saw as one of the most important, if not the most important, aspects of the liberation struggle. This is why he strongly condemned the practice of dishonest acts, abuse of authority, sexual exploitation, and greed for material things. Finally, he highlights the existence or survival of tribalist feelings. Here is Cabral's conclusion in this regard:

> We must be aware of the fact that mistakes on a political and moral level are much more important than those we make on the level of the armed struggle.

Moral behavior is considered as decisive for the good or bad fulfillment of duties. But it is not enough to enumerate instances of misconduct, it is also necessary to seek to understand their deep roots.

The Political Roots of Misconduct

Is this a crisis of growth? Cabral answers this question by considering that the great development of the struggle and the Party created new problems both of a military and political nature, but also, socially, economically, and culturally. The vast majority of the leadership did not have the possibility or desire to keep up with the pace and growth of the struggle through their own training by advancing their knowledge, studying, and becoming aware of experiences already lived. Diverse attitudes and reactions then emerged: confusion (especially on the part of those who played a decisive role during the first phase of the struggle) and the internalization of complexes manifested in various ways, even though commendable adjustments were made to improve training and extract useful lessons from the past.

> It is these differences in training, in reaction to the new and complex difficulties arising in the struggle, and the ever-increasing demands of the fulfillment of daily duties justify our political and military errors, failures, and deficiencies.

Cabral uncovered the *causes* of those errors and indicated the means to eliminate them. Many militants did not give due importance to all aspects of the struggle and instead tended to dedicate themselves to the armed aspect—and even then, only superficially. This revealed a lack of in-depth political knowledge and general awareness. There was a lack of study and concentration, as well as a lack of serious discussion of the problems of life and the struggle. Cultural and political exchange took place within the closed circle of the PAIGC leadership, which meant that there was no *circulation* of ideas and mobility in militants' training.

Party cadres, whether political or military, must take advantage of every opportunity to learn, always learn: learn from their own experience and that of others, learn from books, from life, and from the people.

Moral Roots

Cabral notes that most of the young cadres had adopted easy habits and an easy way of life in urban centers:

These habits explain the bad behavior of some Party officials, reinforced by the power that our organization gave
them by placing them at the head of our action.

Selective Criteria for Militants and the
Behavior of the Popular Masses

In the beginning, the admission of Party members depended on
verbal promises, patriotism, and the will of the candidates. It is
through the struggle itself that selection operates; struggle acts as
a revelator. Men distinguish themselves from one another but they
transform themselves too.

In Cabral's view, the factors of change in the people's support for
the liberation struggle depended on the behavior and mistakes made
by some leaders of the Party and the armed forces.

Its Main Strengths

When finally extracting his general conclusions, Cabral summarized
the axes of the liberation struggle in five points:

a)   the certainty of fighting for a just cause;
b)   the material and human resources available;
c)   the solidarity, decisive in certain aspects, of the African
      peoples, of the progressive and anticolonialist forces of
      the world, and in particular of the socialist countries;
d)   the heroic combat, increasingly important in its devel-
      opment, led by the people of Angola and Mozambique;
e)   the Party organization that dominates all other
      strengths.

These are the characteristics of the armed struggle that define it as a
revolutionary war of national liberation.

IV. Counterpower or the Creation of the
New Society in the Liberated Regions

On several occasions, Cabral had stated his conviction that the greatest success of the liberation struggle lay in the fact that, as the fighting
was taking place, the Party was creating a new social and cultural life

in the country. The *liberated* area consisted, first and foremost, of an objective reality imposed by the evolution of military operations.

Since the end of 1963, the consequences of the guerrilla war included the paralysis of economic exploitation by the colonial power thanks to the elimination of the taxes levied over vast areas, the capture of the main freight transport stations, and the sabotage of terrestrial communication infrastructure. All this had forced the enemy to retreat and to confine itself to a limited number of urban centers in southern and central southern areas of Guinea-Bissau. After six months of armed struggle, almost all of the southern regions of Geba and Corubal had been liberated. These victories were so spectacular that the Portuguese Minister of Defense was forced to publicly confirm their extent by estimating that the PAIGC controlled 15 percent of the country. In the words of an inspired journalist from the *Times* of London, Portuguese Guinea had become "the Achilles heel of Portuguese colonial policy."

The extension of the struggle was accompanied by the strengthening of positions in the liberated regions where, in parallel with the consolidation of the political organization, a new economic structure was being established. The Party sought to maintain and even increase the level of agricultural production, particularly of subsistence products. Hence this important directive from Cabral:

> Consolidate our positions in the liberated regions and develop new structures for our economic, political, and social life in them; train as many cadres as possible; seek the means to accelerate the improvement of the standard of living and the construction of the well-being of our people . . . [115]

Having achieved victory in the Battle of Como, at the moment when the militants were meeting at the First Party Congress, in February 1964, Cabral spoke in his annual report of regions that had been *definitively liberated*. In applying resolutions made at the congress, he mentioned such key political and administrative achievements as "the transfer of power into the hands of local bodies and the creation of special administration committees (state, justice, education, health, etc.)."

The organization of the Party had been entirely restructured and progressively adapted to the dynamics of the process of liberation, proceeding with the creation and installation of base committees that were authentic local bodies for both political and administrative management of the new society being created in the liberated regions. This gave rise to bodies of administration and political supervision at the level of sectors, regions, and fronts. This enabled the masses' participation in the management of their social life.

Taking into account the achievements of the first two years of struggle, Cabral's *Palavras de ordem* directives sought to preserve the spirit of the existing achievements and develop initiatives in the areas of what would come to be known as *national reconstruction*.

At this stage—1965—the situation in Guinea-Bissau was already comparable to that of a state that has part of its national territory, particularly its urban centers, occupied by foreign forces. PAIGC militants would have to retain a fundamental lesson: since struggle or resistance is unleashed on all levels of people's lives, they had to destroy everything that could serve the enemy to continue to dominate the populations, while simultaneously being capable of building everything that could contribute to the creation of a new life in the country.

In this process of *creative destruction*, the PAIGC undertook the entire organization of social life in the liberated regions regarding education, health, the economy, justice, politics, and administration. In essence, it was constructing a *Party-State*.

Cabral's thinking on this matter was dominated by a central idea:

> National liberation, the struggle against colonialism, building peace and progress, independence—all of these are empty and meaningless things for the people if they do not translate into a real improvement in living conditions. There is no point in liberating a region if the people of that region are unable to meet their basic needs.[116]

The liberated regions corresponded, in 1966, to more than half of the national territory (around 60 percent) and were home to 50 percent of the population of Guinea-Bissau.

Given that Portuguese domination could essentially be understood through *cobrança*—the more or less forced imposition of all kinds of taxes—this was no longer possible, even in disputed or partially liberated areas. A concrete and visible example of the fall of the colonial economy was provided by Guinea's main trading company, the Companhia União Fabril (CUF), which had been running a deficit since 1963. This forced it to resort to its reserves to maintain its positions.

Cabral gave the following directives for 1967:

- defend our liberated regions from enemy terrorist assaults to guarantee populations the tranquility essential for productive work;
- study and find the best solutions for the economic, administrative, social, and cultural problems of the liberated regions, increase agricultural production, develop handicrafts, and lay the foundations for the installation of even rudimentary industrial production; continually improve health care and education.[117]

In this *decisive* period, the Portuguese presence became almost exclusively military, as colonial exploitation had been entirely *paralyzed* by the liberation struggle.

In 1969, ten years after the Pidjiguiti massacre, Cabral once again clarified the objective of the *struggle*. It was not just about putting an end to colonial domination, "but," he wrote, it was about "laying the foundations for independence and building the economic, social, and cultural progress of our people, increasingly raising the political consciousness of our populations, creating the essential elements of our sovereignty and security, learning to govern ourselves by governing, allowing our people to have an important part in the management of our lives and to learn, through everyday practice, what well-done work is: organization, freedom, democracy, justice for all, as well as vigilance against all factors contrary to the progress of our country."[118]

In his report of January 1971 (the eighth year of the armed struggle), Cabral highlighted the increase in sufficient production of food crops (rice, in particular) to maintain a constant increase in the pace of the struggle and the benefits acquired by the populations, in large quantities of basic necessities.

Among the important political decisions taken at the internal level, the replacement of interregional committees by National Committees of Liberated Regions (CNRL), which covered the activity of regional committees, was of particular note. The functions of those responsible for national reconstruction were clearly defined, with production being linked to the domain of political action.

In his message of January 1972, Cabral recalled the guiding principles of the PAIGC within the scope of the people's struggle in Guinea-Bissau:

> Our people are aware that the only true compensation for the efforts and sacrifices they have made for the victorious advancement of the struggle lies in a new life of work, justice, democracy, and secure prospects for economic, social, and cultural progress, which we are creating and developing on our land.[119]

Finally, in his last report, written to be presented to the Organization of African Unity (OAU) Council of Ministers on the very day of his tragic disappearance,* he listed a series of indisputable facts in respect to the liberated regions: the existence of a developing state in which the Party has managed to create a new (political, economic, social, and cultural) life; alongside the consolidation of the Party organization, the *development* of the autonomous administration, the *creation* of schools, the installation of field hospitals and clinics, people's courts, an exchange trading system (the people's stores), and other miscellaneous services. He concluded:

> The recent creation, after the general elections by universal and secret suffrage, of the Regional Councils and the first National Assembly of our country is further proof and an important fact of the sovereignty of our people and opens new perspectives for the development of our liberation struggle.[120]

Let us now quickly examine the four domains in which national reconstruction was carried out.[121]

---

* January 17, 1973.

1. Education

The armed struggle for national liberation in its own terms engendered new needs: the training of cadres, the political work of the party, and the administration of the liberated regions. The PAIGC was faced with problems of classification and administration across a relatively vast territorial space.

Since 1960, the old home of Bonfim, in Conakry (in the Republic of Guinea) housed the training school for the first political cadres and a rudimentary primary school.

After the 1964 Congress of Cassacá, the children of Party leaders in combat and war orphans began being grouped together. On January 23, 1965, the current president of the State Council of Guinea-Bissau, Luís Cabral, founded the Escola Piloto, in Ratoma, on the outskirts of Conakry. At the same time, the Instituto Amizade [Friendship Institute] was created to encourage international solidarity.

According to the analysis of one of its first directors, Maria da Luz Boal,[122] the Escola Piloto occupied the summit of a pyramidal system of education and instruction whose base rested on the *tabanca* [village] schools that were spread throughout the liberated regions. This system had some particularities in relation to the methods applied in the usual schools of the time: it emerged as resistance, or rather, as a process, a weapon of transformation and an instrument of creation.

The first phase was represented by bush schools, which educated forgotten children that had been rejected by the colonial education system. The objective was to teach them to read, write, and count without attaching great importance to pedagogical methodology, as the Party's schoolmasters did not have any particular knowledge of the subject. However, it was innovative in certain aspects: the teachers taught militant education and basic political ideas to open horizons of reflection on the rationale for the struggle, on the country, Africa, and the world.

For the 1971–72 school year, the number of students increased to 14,531 in a system with kindergartens and five grades, with 258 teachers for 164 schools.

The sixth grade, created in 1973, included a dozen students at the Conakry Pilot School. The sixth grade of the Teranga school, in Ziguinchor, opened on January 12, 1974 and was intended to welcome child refugees in Senegal, with an initial capacity of 250 students. It should also be noted that 422 cadres were training abroad.

Benefiting from experience and new teachers having passed the entrance exam, the Instituto Amizade [Friendship Institute] developed a new model of pedagogy that was employed first in the Pilot School and then in the liberated regions. It was based on the community life of the children and on the link between agricultural work and education.

2. Health

In *As palavras de ordem*, Cabral stated that health was of the greatest importance:

> Always keep in mind the truth that health is our greatest wealth and the main strength of our fighters and militants. Constantly better health care for wounded and sick combatants as well as activists suffering from any illness; [. . .] develop slowly and according to real possibilities, without compromising assistance to combatants or health care provision to the population of the liberated regions.[123]

If the weight of colonial domination was felt on all levels of social life, it would have had the most disastrous consequences for the health care of the population. Dr. Manuel Boal,[124] then head of the health department, traced the evolution of health organization in the liberated regions in a document drawn up in January 1974.

At the beginning of the national liberation struggle, the objective was very simple: "heal the injured with the means available,"—which was equivalent to moving a mountain with shovels and pickaxes. This is an impressive image that allows us to understand the tasks to be carried out in a situation in which the Party had no doctor and only four qualified nurses. It was necessary to start by selecting a small group that was taught the essential bases of first aid and then placed in combat units and provided with basic materials and some medicines.

This period lasted until 1965. The second stage of growth took place from 1965 to 1970. This involved facing the problems arising from having to administer liberated regions while enduring terrorist bombings by enemy aviation.

The essential objectives of the health department were therefore to ensure better treatment for the wounded, military or civilian, within the liberated regions, to begin the struggle against internal diseases with the means available, to improve the level of medical assistance by installing field hospitals run by doctors and surgeons, and to train health staff on site and, in particular, auxiliary nurses.

These objectives were progressively achieved with the creation of a network of clinics (twenty in 1964, fifty-four in 1965, eighty in 1966) that were spread across the three fronts, and with the opening of the first field hospitals within the liberated regions (two in the north and five in the south) and two rear hospitals in the border cities of neighboring countries: one in Boké, Guinea-Conakry, another in Ziguinchor, Senegal.

From 1970 onwards, the third expansion phase began: the creation of health brigades, efforts to progressively improve the level of treatment provided through the quantitative and qualitative increase in personnel, medicines and equipment of hospital units and others, and finally by the regular launch of preventive health-care campaigns that became routine in 1974.

3. The People's Stores

When characterizing the liberated regions, we previously noted the economic effects produced by combatants' military actions: the capture of barges and other boats belonging to the main colonial exploitation company, the CUF, and the creation of secure conditions for the peasant masses who, freed from threats, could dedicate themselves to the production of their crops. On this basis, PAIGC was able to destroy the groundnut monoculture and free itself from the trafficking economy. In an interview given to the newspaper *Afrique-Asie*, commissar Vasco Cabral[125] described the meaning of the results obtained by the Party in this area:

> First, to break the colonial cycle of groundnut culture which, by extending cultivated areas and reducing fallow areas, has depleted the soil with successive annual crops and irreversibly degraded the land, we relaunched, in the liberated areas, food crops, and tried to diversify them. We took the opportunity to introduce changes to work

methods. At the same time, we developed exchanges, replacing the Portuguese in supplying basic necessities. The people's stores freed the peasants from the coercion inherent to the colonial economy, allowing them to provision themselves and sell their products.[126]

The people's stores, which were based on the barter system (that is, trading food crops for commodities), had had a central warehouse and three intermediaries since 1964. The goods essentially consisted of fabrics, sugar, tobacco, soap, oil, lamps, trinkets, and other products, such as sewing machines or tools. These mostly came from international donations and purchases in neighboring countries or in Europe, in cases of urgent need.

New economic relations began to exist for the rural masses, with surplus products being channeled by the Party, either through *tabanca* committees or the people's stores.

A principle was adopted whereby products were purchased from farmers at a higher price than offered by the Portuguese, while goods that they needed were sold at a lower price.

In 1974, there were five people's stores in the north, eight in the south and four in the east. Self-sufficiency in rice was achieved.

4. Justice

The newly arranged social relations in the liberated regions could not be completed without a true revolution in the administration of justice. Firstly, the colonial justice system, logically characterized by the violence that was inherent to it, had to be broken with. In Guinea-Bissau, formerly subject to indigenous status, only 0.3% of the population (i.e., the *assimilated* identity card holders) were entitled to legal assistance; the vast majority were dominated by arbitrary laws that were applied by administrators and local bosses.

It was not easy to introduce and enforce new laws, considering, on the one hand, the weight of traditions and, on the other, the lack of qualified staff. Hence the conflicts that arose as a result of the dynamics of war. PAIGC's head of justice, Fidelis Cabral d'Almada,[127] considered cases arising from family law to be typical: forced marriage, the obligation to provide a dowry, the separation of spouses or the option of divorce—forms of resistance linked to the problem of women's emancipation. The effort made by the Party to create every possible opportunity for young women, while protecting their cultural personality, collided with the immobile force of backward customs.

Let us consider the evolution of legal regulation. Continuing with an exposition of the same leader, Fidelis Cabral d'Almada, several phases can be distinguished. During the guerrilla warfare period, properly speaking, when the territory was divided into sectors, each guerrilla leader, supported by his group, held all political, military, and judicial power in his zone of control. Cases of the exercise of absolute power were soon found, which enabled repression along the lines of ethnic origin.

After the Congress of Cassacá, we saw the creation of *tabanca* committees within which the people participated in the general administration. By placing justice under the responsibility of the political commissar, the integration of two powers—the judicial and the political—was seen. But the political commissar was doubly limited in his duties and in his field of action. He was ignorant of customary laws due to his urban origins and lacked modern legal training, so could not find fair solutions to conflicts.

With the push for national reconstruction, part of the judiciary power was transferred to the hands of those responsible for production who held economic power. These were not limited to judging property crimes but interfered in the domain reserved for the political commissar, resulting in a conflict of competencies.

In 1969, the Party decided to create the appropriate bodies for the administration of justice.

The only written law was the military justice law, which dated from 1966, but which did not include a civil code. This document, written by Cabral and reviewed by a technical committee led by José Araújo[128] which had given legal form to the Secretary-General's concepts, was essentially a criminal law. Its preamble, however, left a margin of application to civilians. Thus, those responsible for this important sector of social life deepened the study of customary laws as a source of law, with a view to extracting from them the means for resolving concrete cases and inspirations for future laws. The starting point lay in the traditional solution of the conflicts, i.e., the application of the law in the people's courts had its source in customary law. It seemed necessary, without a doubt, to give another tonality to the use of traditional customs in matters of justice, as some of them contradicted the essential principles of the Party. Revelations appeared, for example, in the case of the Balantas, who have a clear vision of justice.

The criteria for choosing candidates for the role of *people's judge* rested on a set of qualities: being a supporter of the Party, a supporter of the new ideas of the revolution, honest and serious, and gathering the consensus of the *tabanca*. Having its own administration through the *tabanca* committee, an armed force distinct from the Party's armed forces (the popular militias) and finally, the courts, the people could exercise triple power: administrative, military, and judiciary.

The popular courts were comprised by three levels:

a) the *tabanca*, formed by three judges, with an essential function of reconciliation: it had a competence in rebus in the application of sanctions without any power to restrict freedom. The popular militia was responsible for ensuring compliance with judgments;

b) the "sector," made up of five people (three members of the Party and two members chosen ad hoc), with the jurisdiction of a court of appeal. Its judgments were final, it had jurisdiction in the application of military justice, but any sentences restricting freedom were limited to four years. It was a civil court that applied the law of military justice, combined with customary law by analogy;

c) the "war tribunal," made up of senior Party officials: the (interregional) political commissar, the head of security, or the military commander, as well as two members chosen by the population. Its competence went beyond the military framework to apply all penalties provided for by law to judge any individual (national or foreign) throughout the liberated territory.

What can be learned from the experiments conducted in the liberated regions?

Was it a simple test in a sociological laboratory?

The historical evolution of events leads to the answer that it was the launch of a new social project. The content of the measures taken in the four areas that we have just briefly described prefigures the contours of the policy followed by the PAIGC. Therein lies, in effect, the projection for the future.

Thus, regarding education, several foreign observers noted the originality of a pragmatic démarche in accordance with the needs of the struggle for independence and combined with the most elaborate pedagogical theories. The Instituto Amizade still serves self-managed educational communities in which a link is established between, on the one hand, agricultural and manual activities, and on the other, education. Likewise, there is a refusal to introduce a rupture between the educational community and the original rural community.

The establishment of a network of health centers, the practice of preventive medicine and the training of medical staff, were principles which guided the leaders who prepared the national health plan once the total conquest of state power had been achieved.

The people's stores were carrying out an original experiment in the commercialization of products. In the beginning, the system was based on exchange, guaranteeing peasants the essential goods that they needed, for their subsistence. They made it possible to develop distribution and supply methods for the populations during the independence phase. Finally, the popular courts within the liberated regions were the bases on which a judicial system open to all layers of society could be created and, together with the rehabilitation centers, the principles of moral recovery.

Part IV.
The Theoretical
Contribution

Cabral constructed a political theory based on the social praxis conducted in Guinea-Bissau and Cape Verde. The formulation of the concepts to be put into practice occurred amid the clash of arms. This rooting in living realities and the intellectual demand of knowing these realities in depth to open the paths to progress, remained Cabral's greatest concern. He critically assimilated everything that had contributed to change in African societies, both in terms of the historical materialism that guided him in understanding the conditions of struggle and other cultural contributions.

Devoid of any dogmatism, Amílcar Cabral's thought was characterized by constant creativity. This was the reason why, in the historic stage of the struggle against imperialism, he innovated across many domains linked to the ideology of national liberation in third world countries.

We must not forget that the process of development of the armed struggle revealed a number of inseparable realities: political orientation; military strategy; the perception of social behavior; the adjustment or restructuring of power; the choice of external alliances. Leadership of this process implies—and this is Cabral's example—the dominance of an ideological reflection whose main lines of force we shall consider.

NINE

Imperialist Domination and the Driving Force of History

Amílcar Cabral's thought, like any living system of thought, evolved through successive deepening. Thus, his formulation of the first fundamental concepts that guided the strategy of the national liberation struggle proceeded, first and foremost, from a historical analysis of Portuguese colonialism, by establishing the necessary link with the international relationship of forces.

The intensive development of capitalism in the nineteenth century led to the first division of the globe, ending with the conquest of raw materials. This is how the main imperialist powers—Great Britain, France, and Germany—used the technical superiority of their means of production to exploit Africa. However, the contradictions of imperialism led to the First World War, then to a new partition that reinforced the British and French positions on the African continent. The victory of the October Revolution and the expansion of the area under socialism called imperialist hegemony into question. The Second World War would decisively influence the destiny of the peoples of Africa.

Cabral, in a text dated 1961, answers the question of how Portugal, underdeveloped and backward, retained its colonies despite the partition of the world. This was mainly thanks to Great Britain, which supported its ambitions—especially after the Treaty of Methuen (1703), which made Portugal into a British semicolony. Interested in economic resources, but also bases of support in the Middle East, Great Britain thus maintained absolute dominance over the Indian Ocean. He added:

The prostitution of African countries dominated by Portugal was a common practice of its colonial policy, in the face of imperialist interests. Only with the support of these interests could Portuguese colonialism survive in Africa. It [Portugal] was not just the jealous guardian of the human and material resources of our countries at the service of world imperialism.[129]

Lenin characterized the various transient forms of dependence for states in the era of imperialism in the following terms:

A somewhat different form of financial and diplomatic dependence, accompanied by political independence, is presented by Portugal. Portugal is an independent sovereign state, but actually, for more than two hundred years, since the war of the Spanish Succession (1701–14), it has been a British protectorate.[130]

At the beginning of the sixties, Cabral already considered that "the greatest difficulties concern the achievement of economic independence—the struggle against neocolonialism." This insight into the analysis of the new mechanisms of domination implemented by imperialist powers in African countries, whose (national and international) sovereignty was granted to them but which then became client states, guides the analysis of the Portuguese situation in light of the unfolding of the struggle in the colonies. This analysis is in line with the resolution on neocolonialism, adopted by the Third Conference of African Peoples and held in Cairo:

[The Conference] considers that neocolonialism, which constitutes the survival of the colonial system, despite the formal recognition of the political independence of the emerging States, which have become the victims of indirect and subtle domination at political, economic, social, military, and/or technical levels, represents the greatest danger that threatens African countries that have recently gained or are near gaining independence.[131]

Cabral has clarified, over the years, his thoughts on this matter and states without leaving room for ambiguity:

> What fundamentally characterizes Portuguese colonialism nowadays is a very simple fact: the Portuguese economic infrastructure cannot afford to engage in neocolonialism.

Hence the following illustration:

> It is from this point that we can understand all the attitudes, all the obstinacy of Portuguese colonialism towards our people. If Portugal had advanced its economic development, if Portugal could be classified as a developed country, we would certainly not be at war with Portugal today.[132]

But Portugal's structural incapacity to practice, through its sole initiative, domination of the neocolonial type does not mean that the Portuguese colonies cannot fall into dependence on exploitation with similar characteristics.

Indeed, Cabral wrote, if it is true that Portugal has not achieved and will not achieve any time soon the indispensable economic conditions for a neocolonialist solution in the territories it dominates, this does not mean that our people are free from this danger. The possibility of installing neocolonialism in our lands comes not only from the imperialist offensive against the real independence and progress of African peoples but also from the contradictions of the African situation.[133]

Cabral defended these ideas during the Second Conference of nationalist organizations of the Portuguese colonies (CONCP) held in Dar-es-Salam in October 1965, which stated in one of its resolutions that "neocolonialism is certainly the main obstacle that the African masses must overcome to realize their aspirations for complete independence."

Parallel to this reflection, Cabral presented Party activists with a pedagogical aside on the nature of Portuguese colonial domination. He stated that colonialism is, above all, economic domination, so as to make people understand the type of exploitation exercised over the masses. Thus, it can be deduced that the first *objective* of resistance and struggle is essentially to liberate the country economically, although it is necessary to *first* undergo political liberation.

Historical evolution demonstrates the veracity of the assertion repeated several times by Cabral: "The Portuguese economic infrastructure never reached a level that could be described as imperialist."

Portugal reaches our times structurally incapable of carrying out a neocolonial policy, which is why it is not in a position—which it would like to be—to begin a "process of decolonization." It is, in reality, a colonialist country, a link in the chain of imperialism, an intermediary in the imperialist exploitation of the African peoples.

Having occupied for a long time a negligible place in the sphere of the European economy, Portugal has sought to integrate itself into this group. It began to give priority to economic growth and particularly to industrial growth. But the traditional dependence of the Portuguese economy on foreign investment would increase its submission to imperialist decision-making centers. Constrained, for thirteen years, to face an increasingly heavy war budget, Portugal had widened its margin of dependence, especially in Angola and Mozambique. In these settlement colonies, where, on the other hand, the extension of the territories and the diversity of (agricultural and mineral) resources made it possible to negotiate the establishment of multinational firms, Portugal tried in vain to promote a neocolonial policy. Even in the extreme hypothesis that this were to happen, it would be an *imperialist condominium*.[134]

Given the traditional characteristics of Guinea's economy and the dynamics of the war imposed by the PAIGC which had taken two thirds of the territory practically the entire countryside—away from Portuguese exploitation, the neocolonial hypothesis has been totally excluded. All this did not prevent the imperialist center, defended by a military alliance, from continuing to support Portugal and providing it with the means to industrialize. "Decolonization" would, in this way, be less profitable for the Portuguese ruling classes than for the imperialist powers.

Subsequent events, starting with the overthrow of the fascist dictatorship on April 25, 1974, illustrated the ideological cohesion and firmness of the positions advanced by Cabral and the member organizations of the CONCP.

However, during his speech at the Tricontinental Conference in Havana, Cabral presented a broader formulation of the concept of imperialist domination, to extract the operational implications aimed at national liberation movements in the Third World.

After historically situating the *fact of imperialism*, "piracy transplanted from the oceans to dry land," he stated that, "both on the economic and social and cultural planes, imperialist capital was, in our countries, far from fulfilling the historical mission carried out by capital in countries of accumulation." However, he made a reservation:

> We must, nonetheless, recognize that in some cases imperialist capital or moribund capitalism had enough interest, strength, and time, in addition to building cities, to increase the level of productive forces, to allow a minority of the native population a better or even privileged standard of life, thus contributing, in a process that some would call dialectical, to the deepening of contradictions within the societies in question. In other, rarer cases, there was the possibility of capital accumulation, giving way to the development of a local bourgeoisie.[135]

Cabral considered the effects of the two general and apparent forms of imperialist domination—direct or classic colonialism, indirect colonialism or neocolonialism—on the social structure and the historical process of peoples. The historical process is frozen in classical colonialism, unlike what happens with neocolonialist domination which "allows the awakening of social dynamics (conflicts of interest in autochthonous social layers or class struggle), [and] creates the illusion that the historical process returns to a normal evolution." This leads to the conclusion that, "the essential characteristic of imperialist domination, both in colonialism and neocolonialism, resides in the denial of the historical process of the dominated people through the violent usurpation of the freedom of development of national productive forces."[136]

The essence of the national liberation of a people then appears clearly: the reconquest of its historical personality, "its return to history, through the destruction of the imperialist domination to which it was subjected." There is, however, a sine qua non for such liberation: "when and only when the national productive forces are completely freed from any and all types of foreign domination."

The foundation of national liberation lies in the "inalienable right of each people to possess their own history," the objective being "the reconquest of this right, which was usurped by imperialism, that is, the liberation of the process of development of national productive forces." Hence the important implication:

> Taking into account the essential characteristics of the world economy of our time, as well as the experiences already lived in the domain of the anti-imperialist struggle, the main aspect of the national liberation struggle is the struggle against what is conventionally called neocolonialism.[137]

There is, therefore, a necessary historical connection between imperialist domination and national liberation.

Cabral also distinguishes the two situations mentioned in relation to sociopolitical practice. The differentiation of the social structure in effect postulates the character of mass organizations: in the colonial situation it is the united front from which the core of the revolutionary vanguard emerges; in the neocolonial situation, it is the constitution of the "true popular vanguard of the national liberation struggle." Cabral also establishes a distinction from the perspective of the struggle: *its outcome* is limited in the colonial case to the nationalist solution, while, in the neocolonial case, "it demands the destruction of the capitalist structure implemented by imperialism in the national territory and precisely postulates a socialist solution."

This is, however, an apparent distinction in time, since "our current historical conditions—liquidation of imperialism, which perpetuates, by all means, its domination over our peoples, and consolidation of socialism in a considerable part of the world—*mean* that there are only two possible paths to an independent nation: the return to imperialist domination (neocolonialism, capitalism, state capitalism), or the adoption of the socialist path."[138]

Cabral did not intend to remake the "science of history," but *to understand it* from a revolutionary point of view in light of the social relations that were to be transformed from a revolutionary perspective.

The essential characteristic of imperialist domination is based on the denial of the historical process of the dominated people. Starting from this thesis, Cabral states that a people subjected to colonial domination cannot have history. Not that its history ceases to exist—which would be absurd—instead, it is blocked, to be placed in the tow of the colonizing state. Therefore, the version of history that denies the history of a colonized people is opposed to the struggle for that people's national liberation.

Cabral introduces a corrective to the famous proposition of *The Communist Manifesto*, "The history of all hitherto existing society is the history of class struggles."[139] He considers that it is worth broadening this thesis and giving it a wider field of application, "taking into account the essential characteristics of certain colonized peoples, that is, those dominated by imperialism."

This situates the debate in the *period* that precedes the division of society into classes and what follows the abolition of class, to admit that it will be more correct to define the *real and permanent engine* of history in these terms: "The level of productive forces is the determining and essential element of the content and form of the class struggle." Cabral comes close to what constitutes the fundamental datum for Marx, that is, the antagonism between the level of productive forces and the pattern of ownership of the means of production, an antagonism that takes shape precisely in the class struggle.

In this way, Cabral's formulation is inspired by the theoretical developments elaborated by Marx and Engels after the publication of the *The Communist Manifesto*, according to which the productive forces are, ultimately, the determining factors of history.

Thus, Engels, in his work *Ludwig Feuerbach and the End of Classical German Philosophy* (1886), when searching for "the driving forces that [. . .] are located under the motivations of the historical actions of men and which constitute in fact the ultimate driving forces of history," he writes, with a certain degree of nuance:

> It is therefore proven that, at least in modern history, all political struggles are class struggles, and that all emancipatory class struggles, despite their necessarily political form—because every class struggle is a political struggle—revolve, in the last analysis, around economic emancipation.[140]

TEN

The Social Lever of the Liberation Struggle

Regarding the formulation of this concept, Cabral began by making a significant effort to free himself from the shackles of dogmatism and ideological mimicry. It is worth remembering that Cabral attempted his first draft analysis of social forces in 1957. At that point, he attributed the role of leading the national liberation struggle to the *proletariat*. As a result of the social unrest concentrated in urban centers, and particularly in Bissau where unrest was tragically illustrated by the Pidjiguiti massacre, the September 19, 1959 meeting of PAIGC leaders decided to reorient the fight against colonialism from the countryside. Some time after the armed struggle began, Cabral was already able to clearly establish the distinction between *main physical strength* from the point of view of confrontation with the enemy—the peasantry—and *the most important* from an historical point of view—the proletariat.

> The strongest class, the main one from a historical point of view [. . .] is, in our opinion, despite everything, made up of [. . .] employees [. . .] of the boats, the factories, the colonial administration, such as the petite bourgeoisie, like me, and others who have a revolutionary consciousness and committed themselves very early on to the people's struggle.

Cabral had deepened the analysis of social stratification and defined the position of the different social groups in the face of the liberation struggle. In effect, this was a question of identifying, based on this political praxis, the reasons which objectively put the different components in a position to take part in such an action and, subsequently, to understand the evolutionary nature of their behaviors.

By examining the social role of the peasantry—or more precisely the *special layer* of the peasantry—Cabral did not minimize the distinction between the differences of classes and therefore of exploitation in certain ethnic groups—the Fulas and the Mandingas—while among the Balantas and other related groups there is an absence of classes (horizontal society), all of this having been shaped throughout the colonial period. So the main *internal* contradiction was located "between the ruling classes (Fulas, Manjacos, etc.) and all the others." Given that it was a colonial society and the type of economic exploitation it engendered, the role of the peasantry in the production of wealth in Portuguese Guinea was fundamental.

Apart from a minority group (among the Balantas), made up of small landowners, no layer of the Portuguese Guinean peasantry was capable of playing a driving role in triggering the liberation struggle, much less of assuming the interests and demands of the other exploited layers. In urban centers, the *driving forces* were: sectors of senior and middle civil servants, independent professionals, small civil servants and commercial employees with or without a contract, small agricultural owners, salaried workers, *déclassés*, and the subgroup of the African petite bourgeoisie or the revolutionary petite bourgeoisie.

In his speech at the seminar organized by the Frantz Fanon Center in Milan (1964), Cabral raised for the first time the question of what would be, at the beginning of the struggle against colonialism, and at the end of its domination, the history-bearing class. He gave a partial answer in these terms:

> We must make a distinction between colonial history and that which belongs to us as human societies: as dominated peoples, we form a group in the face of the oppressor. But when—despite the different influences suffered due to the sometimes-absurd geographical limits that colonialism imposed on us—a class consciousness develops, it can then be said that all social layers are bearers of history. It is impossible, in our colonial context, for a single social layer to carry out the struggle against colonialism, because this would require the effective achievement of national unity.

However, the absence of a social class that drives history could be synonymous with a vacuum; this is not the case. In fact, I have to repeat that it is the colonial State itself, more than the class struggle, that drives history. The important thing is to know who will be able, once colonial power is destroyed, to take the State apparatus into their own hands.[141]

Faced with an illiterate peasantry without direct relations with the colonial forces, an embryonic working class, and the absence of an economically valid bourgeoisie, there remains a social layer "formed in the service of colonialism itself [. . .], the only one capable of directing and using the instruments used by the colonial State against the people: the African petite bourgeoisie."

But how can this *class* be delimited? Is it strictly a class, a layer, or a social category? According to Cabral's interventions, the petty bourgeoisie, in a colonial situation and in the particular case of Guinea, brings together fractions or sectors from other layers and professional categories: civil servants, members of the liberal professions, hired commercial employees, small agricultural owners. It is not, therefore, the notion of a class defined by Lenin as the petite bourgeoisie, which was constituted in the historical conditions of Russia by individual producers and populist or revolutionary socialist intellectuals who expressed the tendencies of that class.

> As for the African petite bourgeoisie, we can define three subgroups: the group committed or even deeply committed to colonialism, which encompasses the majority of senior and middle civil servants and the liberal professions; the group that we call, without great legitimacy, the revolutionary petite bourgeoisie, because from the idea of nationalism it advanced to national liberation; and, finally, the intermediate group, which constantly oscillates between liberation and the Portuguese.[142]

From the point of view of the place it occupies in production, the petite bourgeoisie is not a layer that owns the means of production. Its essential characteristic in relation to other layers of colonized society comes not so much from its economic power, but above all from its intellectual power, as well as its ideological, cultural, and political influence. This power extends through behavior and an aspiration to be rooted in the material comfort of social advancement. Cabral explained:

> We formed [. . .] a group of petite bourgeois and we undertook this struggle as a reaction against our own reality and also because of the influence that events in Africa and the rest of the world had on us and in particular because of that which some of us had been able to endure in Europe, in Portugal and elsewhere. . . .[143]

As Yves Benot notes, the petite bourgeoisie that Cabral speaks of is not a class, "but a group of intellectuals that must constitute itself as an *intelligentsia* of the working class in formation. If these intellectuals orient themselves ideologically in another direction, they can only, as intellectuals, become the *intelligentsia* of this bureaucratic caste interested in business, the ad hoc instrument of neocolonialism. In both cases, they are never, in themselves and as such, a constituted class, and the choice between the two orientations remains a matter of morality—and of individual reflection."[144]

Cabral's concerns are reflected in Mahjemout Diop's analysis of the relations between class and power in Mali:

> Thus, in several black African countries, a layer of wage earners, the intelligentsia, used other employees (office employees and workers) as a maneuvering force to take power . . . intelligentsia rulers are a bureaucratic caste with a strong petit-bourgeois inclination, with all that this entails in terms of inconsistency, hesitation, rash retreats, but also radicalism, leftism, adventurism . . . Here, in Mali, in this so-called decolonized Africa of the 1960s, one should not ask for the impossible, unless one accepts Cabral's idea of a certain class suicide of the revolutionary petite bourgeoisie.[145]

Cabral's position is generally accepted according to which, during the period of the anticolonialist struggle, at a well-defined phase in the level of development of the productive forces, the petite bourgeoisie is a layer that brings together categories of salaried workers who occupy a place in agriculture and commerce, and above all, in the administrative apparatus of cities. It is the supplier of the cadres and its most conscious core (the *intelligentsia*) placed in the lead in political and trade union struggles, making the peasant masses join the liberation struggle.

After the seizure of state power, during the management of national independence, the *ambivalence* of the petite bourgeoisie reveals itself in all its breadth. And it is in this context that one must understand the alternative that, in Cabral's expression, the petite bourgeoisie is faced with: betraying the revolution or committing suicide as a *class*.

To fully play its role in the struggle for national liberation, the revolutionary petite bourgeoisie must be capable of committing suicide as a class, in order to resurrect itself as a revolutionary worker, entirely identified with the deepest aspirations of the people to which it belongs.

Cabral saw this *specific* fatality as one of the weaknesses of the national liberation movement.

Cabral slightly *forced* the metaphor of the petite bourgeoisie's "suicide," which he did not strictly consider as a class. This did not prevent him from having *innovated* intellectually by reestablishing the role of the petite bourgeoisie in leading the national liberation movement in Third World countries.

ELEVEN
The Role of Culture

When we examine the major historical stages that mark Cabral's life and work, we are surprised by the preeminence of the cultural factor. Having modeled his own intellectual personality to the rhythm of the critical assimilation of the world's revolutionary experiences, Cabral carried out the *pedagogy* of national liberation on the twin planes of politics and culture. Seen from the inside, captured from the point of view of the activists in question, Cabral's thoughts spread, in effect, like a penetrating lesson in African culture. In 1949, it was already a matter of making the reality of Cape Verde known to Cape Verdeans themselves; later, at the same time, in Lisbon, there was the fight for *re-Africanization of minds*; finally, during the political battles from the mid-fifties onwards, culture was always at the center of their action. Praia, Lisbon, Bissau, Luanda, and the deep ground of war-torn Guinea are the places where the political-cultural osmosis was elaborated.[146]

Placed at the center of the sociopolitical totality, in a short decade of armed struggle for national liberation, the Party engendered the acceleration of *cultural time* for the people of Portuguese Guinea and Cape Verde, identifiable by these two realities: the gestation of nations and the emergence of states. Thus Cabral, when defining the fundamental characteristic of culture as an essential element of the history of a people, tells us that culture is "perhaps the result of history, as the flower is the result of the plant. It plunges its roots into the humus of the material reality of the environment in which it develops."[147]

121

Even better, culture maintains dialectical relations with history:

> As with the flower on a plant, it is in culture that the capacity (or responsibility) for the elaboration and fertilization of the germ resides, which guarantees the continuity of history, guaranteeing, at the same time, the perspectives of the evolution and progress of the society in question.[148]

Starting from the fact that the cultural resistance of the African people constitutes a permanent and indestructible factor, Cabral defines the liberation movement as "the organized political expression of a people's culture in struggle." This is explained in simpler terms: "By taking up arms to fight for their liberation, our people first expressed their refusal to accept a foreign culture." The realization of this idea required a rational and patient démarche, all directed towards the emergence of the new *social being*. The preliminary phase—that of mobilization—by allowing contact to be established between the different social categories of the population, heralded this sociocultural osmosis. But to achieve this it is necessary to carry out an analysis of the cultural characteristics of each social category, depending on the imperatives of the struggle.

The experience of the liberation struggles in Angola, Guinea, and Mozambique teaches us that the success of political action (or, simply, the commitment of the masses) on the combat fronts which were successively opened up was obtained thanks to an understanding of the populations' own cultural values. Taking into account the diversity of social origins and the differences in level of culture between the protagonists in the theater of struggle, the role of the liberation movement is to correctly delimit these living realities and determine the purpose it proposes to achieve.

The liberation movement conducts cultural work, through the knowledge and awareness it takes not only of the motivations for the struggle (resulting from the oppressive situation in the colonial framework), but also of the contours of ethnic realities. Between intellectuals and peasants, activists from the city and those from the countryside, despite the initial diversity, a common attitude, there was a common *cultural* behavior.

It was found that culture is the true basis of the liberation movement, and that the only societies that can mobilize, organize, and struggle against foreign domination are those that preserve their culture. This, whatever the ideological or idealistic characteristics of its expression, is an essential element of the historical process. It is there that resides the capacity (or responsibility) to elaborate or fertilize elements that ensure the continuity of history and determine, at the same time, the possibilities of progress or regression of society [. . .] Likewise—and because a society that truly frees itself from the foreign yoke returns to the upward paths of its own culture—the liberation struggle is, first and foremost, an act of culture.[149]

The liberation movement that triggers the armed struggle must control the direction of its action in the field of culture until its ultimate consequences. In fact, due to its internal dynamics, armed struggle acts as a revelator of cultural behaviors. Tangible results are located at three levels: self-rehabilitation of cultural values of the peasant masses, agony of elitism, and openness to universality.

These results unfold in practical terms, according to a process that could be presented schematically as follows: the people, once guardians of their traditions, find the social framework for free cultural expression and assimilate, along the way, ideas and new techniques conveyed by the political-military organization, the party. The revolutionary petite bourgeoisie who had previously led the fight for the re-Africanization of minds learn ways of thinking, conceptions, language, and expression from the humble layers of the masses which allow their reintegration into African community life.

This cultural exchange that the struggle imposes and makes possible proves to be of great richness. For the populations of the villages (in the case of the rural guerrilla forces), cultural life expands under the double sign of tradition and modernity, while for the cadres—generally *assimilated* intellectuals from the social categories privileged by the selective game of the colonial system—the cultural space is organized around the harmonious development of a new personality. Only those who have experienced this phenomenon of sociocultural integration in the interior can understand all the implications resulting from it on a psychological level and its consequences on an operational level.

The purpose of the political action led by the liberation movement is to bring about this *new man*, victorious over the alienating constraints of colonial domination, restored to his own history, bearer of universality.

Relying on their own resources, under the stimulating effect of revolutionary war, people reveal their ingenuity and capacity for invention. All artistic creation and all social life are permeated with a powerful affirmation of collective values: the strengthening of bonds between individuals committed to the same liberation struggle, the awareness of the same ends and the same social, political, and cultural tasks create new unitary values and thus become ferments of national consciousness.

This is the reason why Cabral considers the liberation struggle as a factor of culture:

> Whatever its form, the struggle requires the mobilization and organization of a significant majority of the population, the political and moral unity of the various social categories, the progressive elimination of the vestiges of the tribal and feudal mentality, the refusal of rules and social and religious taboos incompatible with the rational and national character of the liberation movement, and brings about many other profound changes in the lives of populations. This is all the more authentic as it is certain that the dynamics of the struggle also require the practice of democracy, criticism and self-criticism, the growing participation of populations in the management of their lives, literacy, the creation of schools and health services, the training of cadres from peasant and worker circles, and many other achievements that imply a true forced march of society in the path of cultural progress. It is thus demonstrated that the liberation struggle is not just a cultural fact, but also a factor of culture.[150]

The selection of cultural values truly takes place within the framework of the struggle, in the fire of the realities lived together by the different social categories and in the face of the solutions to be given to the problems raised by this confrontation. Conflicts soon appear between the modern demands of the struggle and the backward forms and archaic modes of thought inherited from tradition. These cultural weights come from several *regressive* factors from the past: the superstitions on which the magical mentality is based; religious prohibitions, the cult of the sacred tree, for example; customs linked to the family, namely the practice of dowry; the permanence of supernatural rites and beliefs, the wearing of amulets; the various taboos in force in certain ethnicities relating both to some family members and to some foods, and so on. The simple statement of these facts suggests the efforts that the liberation movement must undertake to utilize all human potential in the space of war and harmoniously integrate the cultural values of the people in the pursuit of modern progress.

Cabral attributed particular importance to *cultural resistance* in order to progress in the struggle in Guinea-Bissau. He gave directives in this regard: "eliminate colonial culture and the negative aspects of our own culture, liquidate it in our spirits, in our own ranks; create a new culture based on our traditions, respecting today's achievements that can serve man."[151]

General guidance was also provided: "Conserve what is really useful and constructive, but, little by little, change our clothing, our eating habits, our way of singing and dancing and above all our way of relating to nature, and even our way of relating to each other."

Cultural resistance in the colonial past, in other words, during the phase that preceded the outbreak of national liberation movements, plays a globally positive role, as it is the center of refuge in which African people draw inspiration and creative energies in their determination to struggle against foreign domination. We have just seen that it is enriched with new content in the inevitable confrontation between the traditional values of the past and those dictated by modern progress in the course of the armed struggle. And beyond this aspect, it simultaneously translates into the destruction of the harmful influences of colonialist culture, the creation of new ideas and values engendered by political action (dignity of the people, patriotism, national consciousness), and the development of culture on the scientific basis.

This is the reason why Cabral, when formulating the main objectives of cultural resistance, advocated:

The development of a popular culture and all positive indigenous cultural values [. . .], a national culture based on the history and achievements of the struggle [. . .], a scientific, technical, and technological culture compatible with the demands of progress [. . .], the development of a universal culture on the basis of a critical assimilation of humanity's achievements in the fields of art, science, literature, etc., with a view toward perfect integration into the current world and the prospects for its evolution.

At this point, he concluded:

The achievement of these objectives is, in fact, possible, since the armed struggle for liberation under the concrete conditions of the lives of African peoples facing the imperialist challenge, is an act of fertilizing history, the maximum expression of our culture and our Africanness. The struggle must be translated, at the moment of victory, into a significant leap forward in the culture of the people who are liberated.

In the very development of the national liberation struggle, as the *vanguard* party assured the group of militants' relative stability, and as a new developing society was structured with its state apparatus, the class phenomenon emerged and, therefore, so did class antagonisms. If it is important to seek—when analyzing the political behavior of activists—the class point of view, without falling into the automatism of the coincidence of *social being as ideological being*, it is imperative to adjust and know that this rational approach must take into account, in our case, the characteristics of African man at this stage of his history.

And it is in this sense that Cabral deepens the correlation between mental structures and political behaviors, to explain the essence of certain phenomena, such as the betrayal of the revolution. Hence the importance he attributes to the study of concrete manifestations of aspects of African culture, in confrontation with the modern world: the weight of past beliefs, fear of nature, the influence of a *magical mentality* and the complex of *organic security*. Manifestations that are characteristic of "our weaknesses" and typical of the bio-sociological framework of African man. Insisting on the notion of magical mentality, Cabral takes away all the consequences it engenders in terms of political behavior. The capacity for betrayal depends, in fact, on moral behavior and the firmness of ideological positions. But Cabral confesses that he had not answered certain questions on this matter:

> There is still one more question to ask . . . will it make sense to speak of the Party, of its principles, of its ideology in our historical, social, and cultural living conditions? Here is a question that remains unanswered. We will see. We would say that we are facing a large river full of waves or storms, with people trying to cross and drowning, but they have no other way out: they have to cross . . . Perhaps we will find a path that we can cross more easily: this is the great drama of Africa's liberation struggle.

Appendices

How We Carried Out the Assault on the Management of the Commercial and Industrial Employees Union*

After preparatory work carried out from mid-1956 until the end of that year, we mobilized employees from commerce and industry in Bissau, in other urban centers, and in other locations in the interior of the country where there were branches of the main commercial houses and companies in Guinea-Bissau. In January 1957, we were prepared to carry out an assault undertaken by African union members on the management of the Union of Commercial and Industrial Employees.

It took a lot of audacity and courage for us Africans to direct an operation of this kind—which is easy to understand given the particular conditions of Portuguese colonial society in 1957.

In these elections, we presented the list that had circulated six months earlier in Bissau and in the interior of the country, and we fought to remove the one that had been officially presented by the union and had been dictated by the Portuguese colonial authorities. In the presence of several individuals sent by the Portuguese colonialists to control these elections, João Rosa, Elisée Turpin, Luís Cabral, and I fought to remove this list that went against the interests of Africans and to impose our own. We had a resounding victory—an overwhelming majority. Faced with this fact, the colonial authorities had no choice but to accept our legally valid victory.

This was a huge surprise for the union and employers' leaders, as in previous elections the defenders of employers' interests had always

---

* Report by Abílio Duarte, Minister of Foreign Affairs of the Republic of Cape Verde, collected by the author in Conakry in June 1973.

won. This gave rise to the movement to reestablish the rights of industrial commerce employees within the union.

The statutes themselves stated that fifteen days after the elections the governor of the colony would ratify them; three months passed without any ratification being made. Despite a psychological campaign launched by employers' groups and PIDE (Polícia Internacional e de Defesa do Estado [International and State Defense Police]),[152] we ended up taking over the management of the union.

By the way, PIDE did not exist officially, but instead through the administration service and the Military Command. There were employees who performed these functions, and as they were taken by surprise, they tried to scare us off, but we remained calm and had enough courage to remove the official lists produced by the Portuguese colonial administration and introduce our own, which defended the interests of African employees working in commerce and industry.

The new management included João Rosa, myself, Luís Cabral, and Elisée Turpin, precisely those who had taken the initiative to trigger this union movement.

Comrades João Rosa and Luís Cabral took their places within the General Council of the Union, and I took mine within the management, with the transfer of powers made in the palace by the governor himself in April 1957.

With initial enthusiasm, we decided to review the union's articles and remove from the archives all the cases that had been shelved and analyze them. We had the legal consultant (Dr. Colaço from Goa), who had never had the opportunity to really do his job, and we fought seriously to improve the situation of employees in commerce and industry. This aroused dissatisfaction among employers, who decided to launch a struggle against the new union management that was threatening the exploitation structure so long in place.

Due to all the obstacles that were placed before us, we reached the end of the year without having achieved much and did not stand for reelection. We left the union and began, with right on our side and with more arguments to back ourselves up, to struggle within the Party's clandestine structures—the only possible way to defend the interests of our people.

What then happened was exactly what we had predicted. A deeper awareness began to take root of the fact that it was not possible to truly defend the essential interests of the people through the structures of the colonial administration. There was a need to find another path, a path that had already been outlined by the party—the clandestine struggle to trigger the armed struggle.

This led to many who had been unable to accept that we were capable of fighting against Portuguese colonialism to begin to believe that something could be done. And this idea was profoundly reinforced with the events of August 3, 1959.

The First Party Meeting*

[. . .] Back then, I, Comrade Aristides Pereira, and others lived in a shared house, but only he and I were close. We were already close politically, culturally, and professionally (since we both worked at the post office). We had cultural contacts and—secretly—political contacts with the current president Luís Cabral, who often received a French newspaper and magazines that sometimes arrived in such a state that they didn't even have a name. They came in envelopes and we passed them on to other comrades inside of books. We already had contacts with Comrade Amílcar Cabral, who attended some meetings, corrected us on many aspects, and drew our attention to the guidelines that we should follow in our work—but with great caution. After some time, in conversation, he had some contact with Comrade Aristides whom he had known for a long time and so we arranged a meeting. When I arrived at home, I was informed by Comrade Aristides that we had a meeting to discuss an important matter. He asked me if I was ready for this and I replied that I was, but that there was a question of me still engaging in collaboration with the MLG [Liberation Movement of Guinea]. He said it was a problem we were going to raise and we did. We had the meeting, I presented the situation that I was in to Comrade Cabral, he understood and agreed: from that moment on, we six decided to form the Party. That is how we decided on the Party formation and decided to take an oath to give our own lives, if necessary, for the realization of the supreme ideals that could

---

* Report by Fernando Fortes, published in *Nô Pintcha*, September 18, 1975.

be summed up as doing everything to achieve the independence of Guinea-Bissau, and to do everything in our power to achieve the independence of Cape Verde, and then to make the two peoples decide their destiny; reciprocally, of course.

But we were initially convinced that we could, through political work and enlightenment, gradually infiltrate certain organizations.

There was indeed a document, but at this exact moment I have the impression that it no longer exists because it was in the Bissau archives. The document essentially contained an oath to the effect that we were authentic Party militants and, if necessary, would give up our own lives. We committed ourselves to giving all our effort and all our intelligence to defend the highest interests of the Party, whose statutes Comrade Amílcar Cabral had already outlined, but there was no time to clean up due to that situation.

[. . .] The meeting took place in the evening, in the house whose owner was a bank employee and the residents were Comrade Aristides Pereira and another young man who must be in Argentina at the moment. The three of us lived in the same house. Sometimes my brother would visit and there was also a young man who used to come by—Jorge de Carvalho—a very good friend and schoolmate of Comrade Aristides, killed by the PIDE in Angola. They were all trustworthy, so much so that there were trustworthy people in the neighborhood so that when we got together there was one outside. We even had a prearranged doorbell signal: when the bell rang, we hid our books and everything else. We also had a way out through the back, but that night there was no problem. We took so many precautions that people were convinced no one was home.

Even our pupil, Comrade Arafan Mané, didn't realize that we were there.

[. . .] The initial core of the party was involved in staff training, through group readings. Comrade Abílio Duarte took part many times. We listened to international news and read newspapers that came to us from Senegal or Guinea-Conakry. There was a division of labor: Comrade Luís was responsible for financial, cultural, and student matters; Comrade Aristides was responsible for foreign relations; I was responsible for internal relations.

The Events of August 3, 1959*

It is possible, today, despite twenty years having past and the disappearance of many important testimonies, to faithfully reconstruct the development of the events that culminated on August 3, 1959 with the Pidjiguiti massacre.

These events were not due to chance, nor to a thoughtless action or a simple unconscious impulse of the oppressed masses. They resulted, rather, from all the political activity previously carried out in our country in the search for effective forms and appropriate paths for a consistent struggle against the foreign occupier and for national independence.

We referenced, in several instances, the strike of February 1956, in which port workers abandoned their vessels for eight days and demanded a salary increase. Some captains were arrested. Nonetheless, the bosses of the owner companies found that the strikers were not giving in and that colonial economic interests resented the paralysis of river shipping. The colonial government was forced to summon the administrators of the large companies—Gouveia, Ultramarina, and Barbosa—to Lisbon so that the problem could be resolved. The movement resulted in a victory for the strikers, who saw their just demands met.

Three years later, in February 1959, to face the increasing cost of living, the sailors who worked on the Casa Gouveia boats asked their employers for another salary increase and obtained an assurance that

*   Statement from the General Secretary, Aristides Pereira, at the symposium on "The Political Significance of the Pidjiguiti Massacre," Bissau, August 1 and 2, 1979.) [This document was not included in the appendix of the French version]

their request would be duly considered. Months passed, however, without any solution emerging. This forced boat and port workers to threaten to strike.

Although the employers then committed themselves more clearly to meeting the demands, no satisfaction was given to the workers, which led them to decide, in secret, to take industrial action.

The strike was initially scheduled for July 31, which was the day they were to receive their salaries. If their demands were not met by then, the crews and loaders of all the river transport vessels that used the Pidjiguiti pier would down tools.

As the Gouveia pay clerk only showed up three days later to pay them the same amount as they had received on their last payday, the leaders of the movement decided to immediately go on strike and communicate the fact to the company manager who, it is worth noting, received a monthly salary of more than twenty *contos*. To quantify this: twenty *contos* is more than the total salaries of two hundred sailors.

In the early afternoon, at a meeting on the pier, the striking workers were summoned by a colonial port official, the chief boss of the Captaincy, to appear at the Gouveia warehouses so that they could receive a raise.

Faced with the bosses' insistence that the sailors receive their usual remuneration at the warehouses, the strikers—who had previously rejected several attempts at bribery and divide-and-rule—[duly went there and] reaffirmed their just demands and determination to continue their strike.

In response to a request from the Gouveia bosses, the police sent a detachment to the location. Their chief officer, aware of the events, addressed the strikers in an arrogant and provocative manner. He even went so far as to attack one of them who, not being intimidated, responded in kind and drove the police officer from the scene.

Once the striking workers returned to the port, police and military reinforcements arrived to support the colonialists. The massacre took place shortly before 4 p.m. on that tragic day of August 3, 1959. The struggle was an unequal one: on one side of the Pidjiguiti pier gate, closed by the colonialists, the sailors and dockers were armed with no more than oars and sticks; facing them were the settlers and their African lackeys—policemen, soldiers, and civilians—armed with machine guns and rifles. In twenty minutes, with the hatred and fury typical of murderers, the colonialists shot dead fifty strikers and injured more than a hundred. They also shot many who, in desperation, tried to escape by throwing themselves into the water. Some of these workers were honored by the heroic gesture of one sailor, Ocante Benunte, a PAIGC member, who threw himself into the river and swam to a boat, later using it to transport them to Bandim.

Once the massacre was complete, the survivors, before being taken to the dungeons of the Santa Luzia Barracks, where they were held for several months, were forced to carry the bodies of the fallen workers in trucks that transported them to the hospital mortuary, under close military surveillance. Only the sailors' wives were allowed to watch over the bodies of their husbands. Traditional mourning ceremonies were banned.

The African population of Bissau, who had watched the massacre in horror, were prevented from approaching the scene of the crime by a strong detachment of colonial troops. This meant that they had to contain their indignation to avoid further loss of human life. On the night of August 3, the alarmed colonialists sent soldiers and police into the streets of the capital to guard strategic locations and prepare to brutally crush the merest hint of revolt.

There were arrests, beatings, torture, and abuse of all kinds against parts of the population considered suspect. A wave of the most barbaric terrorist repression invaded poor neighborhoods and threatened an even greater bloodbath. This was only prevented because PAIGC leaders and workers knew how to curb any action by the most outraged parts of the community and calm the overall population, who wanted to express their indignation en masse. Thanks to their quick actions, the African people of Bissau, unarmed as they were, did not fall foul of the criminal trap laid for them the Portuguese colonialists and their miserable agents.

The FLGCV Charter

I.   Anticolonial political organizations from so-called Portuguese Guinea have decided to form an organic united front under the name: The Guinea and Cape Verde Liberation Front (FLGCV).

II.   The Front is open to all political parties and anticolonialist mass organizations created by Guineans, Cape Verdeans, or to Guineans and Cape Verdeans in Guinea, on the Cape Verde Islands or overseas.

III.   The Front adopts the political line defined in the political program of the African Independence Party (PAI—Guinea and Cape Verde), an autonomous political organization created in so-called Portuguese Guinea by Guineans and Cape Verdeans.

IV.   The Front's objective is the immediate conquest of the independence of so-called Portuguese Guinea and the Cape Verde islands. In the struggle for national independence of the Guinean and Cape Verdean peoples, the Front will use peaceful means but will respond effectively to all violence used by Portuguese colonialism to maintain its domination.

V.   The direction of the Front is ensured by the PAI's higher bodies, which include the main leaders of other member organizations.

VI.   The Front may only be dissolved when its objective has been fully achieved.

— Signed Abel Djassi [a.k.a. Amílcar Cabral]
Bissau, September 19, 1959

Conclusion

The Current Place of Amílcar Cabral's Political Ideas

As a revolutionary leader, Amílcar Cabral dedicated himself in particular to making Party members and the people of his country understand the profound meaning of independence. His political pedagogy encompassed all domains of national life, which unfolded in the din of arms at the same time that the components of the developing state were forged in the liberated regions. In his numerous interventions at meetings and conferences of cadres, Cabral not only clarified the content of national independence, but also defined in detail the main guidelines that the state power in Guinea-Bissau and Cape Verde should follow. The field of sovereignty was covered by pertinent reflection, whether it be the political, social, economic, cultural, or diplomatic aspect. Using the study of concrete cases drawn from the experience of African countries subjected to neocolonial domination, Cabral was able to indicate examples to avoid. And, addressing the fighters of the third world, he had deepened in his theoretical texts— as we have just seen—the broader notion of national liberation, a stage achieved only at the moment when the determinism of the capitalist market ceases to operate.

Since the founding of the State of Guinea-Bissau on September 24, 1973, the PAIGC higher authorities stated, in the preamble of the text of the proclamation, their fidelity to the political line formulated by Cabral: "The State of Guinea-Bissau assumes the responsibility for promoting the country's economic progress, thus creating the material bases for the development of culture, science, and technology, with a view to constantly raising the standard of social and economic life in the country. our populations and for the ultimate realization of a life of peace, well-being and progress for all the children of our land."

However, there are political commentators who question the relevance of political thought developed during the armed struggle for liberation. They ask whether it is possible to find guidelines that allow action to be guided in the present phase, characterized by the effort of national reconstruction and development. The answer to this question was given by the Third PAIGC Congress, which took place in Bissau in November 1977. This Assembly, gathered under the triple sign of *independence* together with *unity* and *development*, clarified the Party's options. There was coherence in the theses presented to the congress, which constituted the foundations of its political and ideological line.

Firstly, the affirmation of PAIGC's Party-Movement duality or, in other words, the permanence of the characteristics of its past—a national front, mobilizing different social layers, but whose leading core had, from the outset, formulated clear objectives to be achieved with a view to the liquidation of colonialism. In fact, no class was alone the bearer of history. That is, no class was capable of assuming exclusively the role of revolutionary vanguard. This is why, we read in the first thesis,

> the historical process of our national liberation struggle was triggered not by a class, but by the revolutionary sector of the petite bourgeoisie that knew how to win over the most exploited working classes to the idea of independence, organize them into a vast movement and integrate the most dynamic elements into the political leadership.[153]

Certainly, new types of relations were created in the societies of Guinea-Bissau and Cape Verde, through the liberation of national productive forces. But it is undeniable that these transformative factors "have not yet produced significant qualitative changes in the class structure." This is the reason why the thesis states bluntly that "the social engines which have led the revolutionary process so far prove to be perfectly suited to current realities." Viewed from the angle of class relations, or in light of the dynamics of social mobilization, the PAIGC defines itself today as a liberation movement in power.

If the essence of national independence lies in the exercise of political power by the people, this power rests, however, on a fragile economic base, due to the low level of development of the productive forces. It is about expanding and consolidating its economic base—which is a priority task. This implies a mobilization of existing national resources and the labor force of the popular masses. Since no class objectively meets the conditions to direct the revolutionary process on its own, the development effort must necessarily be carried out within the framework of a national democracy oriented towards defending the interests of the working classes. A revolutionary democracy in its content and in its profound purpose. The creation of democratic institutions—the popular basis of the State of Guinea-Bissau and which inspired institutions of the same nature for Cape Verde— the intervention of the masses in the sphere of power takes place at all levels of the state structure. As early as 1965, Cabral formulated the principles of revolutionary national democracy, recommending:

> We must increasingly improve the strength of the people, move forward with courage towards the conquest of Power by the people, towards the radical transformation (at the base) of the lives of our people, towards a stage in which the weapons and means of defense of our revolution will be entirely in the hands of the people.[154]

But the achievement of progress and social justice also presupposes the construction of an independent national economy—"a planned economy with secure foundations, balanced in relation to the outside, independent in financial and monetary terms." It is worth noting, in this regard, that the states of Guinea-Bissau and Cape Verde had to face common obstacles, as a result of colonial domination: a high rate of illiteracy, the absence of technicians and intermediate frameworks, a weak transport network that does not correspond to internal regional needs, an almost nonexistent energy network, an almost total non-use of natural resources, inadequate education, and health infrastructures concentrated in urban centers.

To master these realities, PAIGC opted for an accumulation model that tends to break the basic structures of underdevelopment.

In the report presented to the Third Congress, the current Secretary General of the Party, Aristides Pereira, stated that the cornerstone of the development strategy lies in the political action of the PAIGC, which must mobilize all social layers, must occupy every meter of cultivable land, must demand the maximum from each cadre, and must integrate the entire country into a vast national reconstruction effort in order to produce more and produce better.

To overcome factors that slow development, it is imperative, even vital, to boost socioeconomic activities, especially within the country, to avoid the creation of artificial growth poles and disparities that could jeopardize the balanced and harmonious development of the country. The progress of the economy must be based, first and foremost, on internal dynamism, and rely first and foremost on its own strengths.

Taking into account the characteristics inherent to Guinea-Bissau and Cape Verde, the development problem arises in a slightly different way in each of the countries. Thus, in Guinea, two fundamental issues are in the process of being resolved: the creation of conditions for balancing the balance of payments; the need to reinforce and expand measures leading to breaking the closed circuit of self-subsistence, a state in which 80 percent of the population finds itself. Hence the imperative to "give priority to industries essentially focused on the foreign market" or capable of quickly increasing an exportable surplus. In response to the second question, industry and services will be called upon to play an important role.

Industry should tend to satisfy the vital needs of the rural population, in order to produce commodities and place them on the market. Thus, agriculture and industry are linked together in balanced development: agriculture as the base and industry as a dynamic element. Agriculture remains, in fact, the priority sector of the development strategy of Guinea-Bissau. In current conditions, it also constitutes the main productive sector in Cape Verde and brings together the majority of the active population. Despite its unpredictable nature, agriculture plays an important role in development in general and in the economy in particular, above all in reducing food dependence and improving the diet of the population. In the minds of the leadership of the PAIGC, there are only two models of development: the one that reproduces underdevelopment and the one that breaks the latter's basic structures, opening the way to an independent national economy.

Faithful to its primary project, the PAIGC continues to develop its action to bring about unity between Guinea and Cape Verde. This unity is already prefigured in blood ties, the community of historical, ethnic, and cultural formation, as well as in shared experiences lived in the context of socioeconomic complementarity under colonial domination. With the creation of the Party in 1956, the unity consciously accepted by Guineans and Cape Verdeans was consolidated in political praxis. And it was decisive for the success of the armed struggle for national liberation.

The PAIGC Secretary General's report reads:

> The strength of unity resides in the people's awareness of their need, an awareness that develops in the experience lived in common on a daily basis in the process of forming the material, social and cultural bases for its achievement. This dynamic conception of unity, that is, of gradual and safe progress, presupposes a process of complementary development and coordination at the level of power structures, within the framework of a common strategy.
>
> This common strategy must introduce a qualitative change in the cooperation process between the two States. Cooperation will thus come to be understood as the resolution of the needs of both, relying on the potential of both. Given the enormous needs of each State in all sectors and the relative complementarity of their potential, this strategy will allow the optimal use of resources to better meet needs, thus laying the practical foundations of principled unity.[155]

It is in this sense that the various forms of action are coordinated by the main body responsible for bringing about, definitively, the dynamic conception of unity between the states the: *Intergovernmental Conference.* Unity and cooperation are understood as a means to fully achieve the independence and development of both countries, with unity being a requirement for development and an element in the strategy for independence.

Finally, as far as foreign relations are concerned, the PAIGC, which strictly observes the principle of independence of thought and action, maintains international relations based on an ideological reference that presided over the creation of the Party: the liquidation of colonial rule is inseparable from the struggle against imperialism. In the great confrontations that shake the world, the States of Guinea-Bissau and Cape Verde have adopted conduct in accordance with their proclaimed principles, namely that of nonalignment. But, considering that the anti-imperialist factor constitutes the fundamental nucleus of nonalignment, these states prioritize their active support for the struggle toward genuine liberation of the peoples of Africa, the Middle East, Asia, and Latin America.

Rooted in the concrete realities of Guinea-Bissau and Cape Verde, inserted in the social fabric of these two countries, Cabral's thought never ceases to inspire the action of PAIGC leaders. Stating that Cabral's ideas continue to be operational is equivalent to shouting evidence. Because the work of Amílcar Cabral, in effect, defines the essential problem of the content of independence and guides the activists determined to bring about the emergence of societies free from any form of exploitation.

Far from being reduced to a simple *speech* on national liberation, Cabral's writings constitute the theoretical basis on which the revolutionary process set in motion by the States of Guinea-Bissau and Cape Verde rests. And the strict application of this loyalty resides in a tangible fact: the popular masses, particularly in the countryside, already benefit from the most important advantages resulting from the material and social changes carried out in these countries during the years of independence. Achieving balanced, endogenous development, within the framework of a national and revolutionary democracy which will characterize the future State of the Union of Republics in Guinea-Bissau and Cape Verde. This appears to be, definitively, the political testament retained by the followers of Amílcar Cabral's work.

— Bissau, March 1980

Endnotes

Endnotes

Editor's note: Andrade makes numerous references to several key publications of Cabral's work. *Unidade e luta*, originally published in French by Maspero as *Unité et lutte*, was a two volume publication which was later translated into English as *Unity and Struggle* by Monthly Review Press. However, only two-thirds of the original French was translated into English as one single volume rather than two. We have thus indicated where the reader can find the corresponding English references in brackets following the citation of *Unidade e luta*.

Andrade also makes regular citations of Cabral's *Palestras no seminário de quadros*, or Lectures at the Cadre Seminar in November 1969. The entirety of this seminar has been published in portuguese by the Amílcar Cabral Foundation as *Pensar para melhor agir: intervenções no seminário de quadros* in 2014. Sections of the seminar have been published in *Unity and Struggle* (the section titled "Party Principles and Political Practice") and in *Resistance and Decolonization* published by Rowman & Littlefield. 1804 Books is currently preparing the first complete English language translation of the entire seminar.

Generally, endnotes added or significantly edited by the editor of this editions have been marked by brackets. Otherwise, only slight edits for purposes of clarifying some references for the English reader have been made without notice.

Part I. The Emergence of the Unifier

Chapter 1. Roots

1 Juvenal Cabral, *Memórias e reflexões*, Praia, 1947
2 Without a doubt, António Lopes da Costa retained the qualities of the poet Junius Juvenalis (65–128): classical rhetoric, realism, and, above all, the satire that reached its peak with him. See: R. Morriset and G. Thévenot, *Les Lettres latines*, Magnard, 1950.
3 Juvenal Cabral, *Memórias e Reflexões*.
4 The author explains that, at the time Pedro Lopes da Costa lived, monthly fees at the São Nicolau seminary and in Portugal did not "exceed 5,000 to 10,000 *réis*, depending on the financial possibilities of the students' parents or guardians." The sum that he had inherited was ample to cover five years of schooling.
5 See: *Boletim Oficial* n. 31/911 to 5/8/1911.

6   *Boletim Oficial* n. 43. 25/10/1913. Pg. 400.

7   Juvenal Cabral, *Memórias e Reflexões*.

8   Ibid.

9   According to the registry of births (document no. 58, declaration of October 11, 1924, in Bafatá), Juvenal Cabral preferred the spelling "Hamilcar," unquestionably as a means of highlighting his classical erudition and admiration for the famous Carthaginian general of the same name, the great African that shook the Roman empire.

10   Juvenal Cabral, *Entre professores primários: Um caso inédito*, Minerva de Cabo Verde, Praia, 1944.

11   As a former elementary school teacher, Juvenal Cabral received 160,000 *réis* per month from the Retirement and Pension Fund for the Families of Public Servants of Guinea.

12   See: PAIGC declaration presented to the UN special committee by Maria Dulce Almada in June, 1962.

13   *Memórias e reflexões*, op. cit.

14   Ibid.

15   Ibid.

16   Ibid

17   Manuel Ferreira accurately describes this painful aspect of the life of the people of the Archipelago during the Second World War, in his novel *Hora di bai*, translated by Maryvonne and Gilles Lapouge, Casterm.

18   Amílcar's mother would later say, on the subject of the influence Juvenal exerted on her son: "Without a doubt, he was born with politics on his mind. He was the son of a politician . . . Juvenal talked to him about all of these things" (*Nô Pintcha*, No. 225, September 12, 1976). Dona Iva Pinhel Évora, who died in Lisbon on August 11, 1977, was buried in Bissau in an official ceremony.

19   He passed his Elementary School exams on July 22, 1937, according to School Record No. 1230 of the Liceu do Infante D. Henrique, 26/X/1937.

20   In "La machine Singer" a poem from the collection *Poète à Cuba*, Paris, 1876

21   In Aime Cesaire, *Cahier d'un retour au pays natal*, Bordas, 1947, Paris.

22   See: *Palestras no seminário de quadros*, 1969.

23   A classmate from secondary school, Manuel Coutinho de Jesus, now deceased. Information provided by another contemporary, Alcibíades Tolentino.

24   Conversation with Arnaldo França.

25   Praia, September 1943. [The date here likely refers to when Cabral wrote the attributed quote. Much of Cabral's poetry and other creative writings before his political activity is archived at the Amilcar Cabral Foundation]

26   *Boletim da Casa dos Estudantes do Império Mensagem* no. 11, Year II, May–December 1949.

27   These quotes from a certain Abbé de La Roudaire are fitting here: "It won't happen now, perhaps, but the day of Justice and Peace will certainly dawn. There is one people on Earth to whom all the nations belong."

28   Ibid.

29   Cabral's yearbook shows this to be true.

30   Appointed by Ordinance of November 22, 1944

31   Amilcar Cabral, *A Ilha*. Ponta Delgada (Azores), July 22, 1946

Chapter 2. Cultural and Political Education

32 Conversation with the author in Bissau, on June 11, 1976.

33 "Conversation with my Poetry," poem addressed to the magazine *Seara Nova*, which did not publish it.

34 Published in *O Metalúrgico*, the private journal of the CPTOMM sports group, in the issue dated July 15, 1948.

35 Correspondence with Maria Helena Vilhena Rodrigues of August 17, 1948.

36 Ibid.

37 Correspondence of August 20, 1948.

38 Correspondence of January 8, 1949.

39 Léopold Sédar Senghor, *Anthologie de la nouvelle poésie nègre et malgache*, Presses Universitaires de France, Paris, 1948.

40 Correspondence with Cabral.

41 Correspondence of April 15, 1949.

42 Correspondence of July 29, 1949.

43 In his letter dated September 28, 1949, Cabral provided precise details about a skin allergy that had kept him in bed for eight days—the worst days of his mother Dona Iva's life.

44 "Algumas considerações sobre as chuvas ['Some considerations about the rains,']" a lecture delivered by Cabral at the Rádio-Clube de Cabo Verde, on September 8, 1949, text published in *Boletim de Cabo Verde* No. 1, October 1949.

45 Alves Roçadas, card to Cabral, Praia, September 16, 1949.

46 Amílcar Cabral, "Um comentário," Praia, October 1949. The text indicates the date of the broadcast: October 13.

47 *Palestras no seminário de quadros*, [*Lectures at Cadre Seminars*], 1969. [The *Palestras*, or Lectures, were recently published in Portuguese as *Pensar para melhor agir: intervenções no seminário de quadros, 1969* by the Amílcar Cabral Foundation in 2014. They will soon be published by 1804 Books in English].

48 Amílcar Cabral, "Em Defesa da Terra ['In Defense of the Earth Pt. 3']" Cabo Verde, *Boletim de propaganda e informação*, November 1949.

49 Agostinho Neto, "*Confiança*" in Sagrada Esperança, Sá da Costa, Lisboa.

50 The active participation of Vasco Cabral, a student from Guinea-Bissau, at the Faculty of Economics, who was quite experienced in the clandestine dealings of Portuguese democratic movements, was a noteworthy figure here.

51 Cabral participated, for example, in a Portuguese-language adaptation of the play *Le Maitre d'Ecole* [*The School Master*], by Guinean author Fodéba Keïta, the famous creator of Ballets Africains.

52 Francisco José Tenreiro and the author involved drawing up a program outline for the African Study Center. The first version was presented in August 1951.

53 *Présence Africaine*, special edition, "*Les etudians noirs parlent* . . . [*The Black Students Speak*]" No. 14, 1953. A collaborative work (unsigned) from Francisco José Tenreiro, Amílcar Cabral, Agostinho Neto, Mário de Andrade, and Alda do Espírito Santo.

54 *Caderno de poesia negra de expressão portuguesa*, edited by Francisco José Tenreiro and Mário de Andrade, illustration by António Domingues, Lisbon, July 1953.

Chapter 3. Return to the Home Country

55 His scientific bibliography in 1951 includes the following titles: *O problema da erosão do solo* [*The Problem of Soil Erosion*]; *Contribuição para o seu estudo na Região de Cuba (Alentejo)* [*Contribution to your study in the Region of Cuba (Alentejo)*], Instituto Superior de Agronomia, Lisboa; *O conceito de erosão* [*The Concept of Erosion*] ibid., *Um projecto para o estudo dos solos em Cabo Verde* [*A Project for the Study of the Soils of Cape Verde*], Estação Agronómica Nacional, Lisboa (unpublished).

56 *Palestras no seminário de quadros:* "Evolução e perspectivas da luta," 1969.

57 Ibid. Bacar Cassama, currently a member of the State Council and Chief of Staff of the Presidency, confirmed this episode in a conversation with the author in February 1973.

58 Cabral also participated, for the first time, in a scientific conference outside of Guinea. The conference took place in September 1954, in Bambey, Senegal and was known as the "Arachidemils" conference.

59 Diogo de Melo e Alvim had previously been governor of the Mozambican province of Zambézia. In this capacity, he hosted Brazilian sociologist Gilberto Freyre at his residence in Quelimane in January 1952. This gave him his love of travel: "I've already visited almost every country in the world. All that's missing from the list is South America. I never really had the opportunity to visit that wonderful land and turn the dreams that have filled my imagination since childhood into reality. It is therefore not surprising that my greatest wish is that God will one day allow me to visit Brazil, and to feel at home there, as you must feel in Portugal" (in Gilberto Freyre, *Aventura e Rotina*).

60 Mention must be made at this juncture of the Portuguese progressive, Dona Sofia Pomba Guerra, who was a pharmacist and the English teacher at the high school of Bissau, A member of the Communist Party, she sought, apparently without success, to form communist cells among the Guineans. She did, however, play a role in awakening an anticolonial consciousness among some young people, such as her employee Osvaldo Vieira. Vieira, who would go on to be one of the Party's first fighters, was responsible for opening the northern front in 1963 and died in 1974.

61 Later murdered by the PIDE.

62 See the report by Abílio Duarte in the appendix.

63 See the report by Fernando Fortes in the appendix.

64 The acronym PAIGC was adopted in October 1960.

65 Purely by chance, another meeting, this time cultural in nature, took place on the anniversary of the foundation of the PAIGC. This meeting was to be among the most important cultural events of that decade: the opening in Paris of the First World Congress of black writers and artists, organized by the magazine *Présence Africaine*.

66 "We Guineans and Cape Verdeans have been lucky since 1960. That was when I was elected with votes from all our comrades from the Portuguese colonies who were with us, to begin denouncing Portuguese colonialism in the world. In February 1960, we gave our first international press conference in London, during which we unmasked Portuguese colonialism, published the first pamphlet against colonialism, and wrote the first pamphlet against Portuguese colonialism, written by one of the children of the Portuguese colonies," (*Palestras no seminário de quadros:* "Resistência política,"), 1969.

67 *Palestras no seminário de quadros:* "Evolução e perspectivas da luta," 1969.

68 Created in the militant atmosphere of the Conference, it succeeded the MAC (Movimento Anti-Colonialista [Anti-Colonial Movement]).

69 These were Luciano Ndao, Bobo Turpin, and Daouda Bangoura.

70 Whatever our assessment of Morocco's foreign policy after Algerian independence and of the 1963 war between Morocco and Algeria, it is undeniable that Morocco's King Hassan II, African Affairs Minister Abdelkrim Khatib, and Defense Minister Majoubi Aherdane provided decisive assistance to the liberation movements in the Portuguese colonies. A permanent CONCP secretariat was established in Rabat; military training of young combatants in coordination with the ALN (Algeria) [took place on Moroccan territory]; Morocco supplied weapons and ammunition that enabled the PAIGC to undertake direct action in Guinea-Bissau.

Part II. The Weapon of Criticism and the Instruments of Knowledge

Chapter 4. The Formation of Cabral's Political Thought

71 An agricultural system based on periodic exploitation of soils.

72 See: "Notas acerca da razão de ser, objectivos e processo de execução do recenseamento agrícola da Guiné," *Boletim cultural da Guiné portuguesa*, No. 33, 1954; "A propósito da mecanização da agricultura na Guiné portuguesa" ibid., No. 34, 1954; "Acerca da utilização da terra na África negra," ibid., No. 34, 1956; "A agricultura da Guiné, suas características e seus problemas fundamentais," *Agros*, vol. 42, n. 4, 1959; *Unidade e luta, I: A arma da teoria, Seara Nova*, 1976, Chapter "O homem e a terra," pp. 33–56 [*Unity & Struggle*].

73 The meeting, which took place clandestinely in Paris (in his Place de la Sorbonne, then home of Marcelino dos Santos) from November 15 to 18, 1957, was attended by Amílcar Cabral, Viriato da Cruz, Guilherme Espírito Santo (all three now deceased), Marcelino dos Santos, and Mário de Andrade.

74 In summary, according to the notes we kept.

75 And he adds a note about the evolution of the mentality and behavior of the Cape Verdean element: while in the past Cape Verdeans were used to serve in the Portuguese occupation and domination in Guinea, now they tended to get closer to the people and participate in the struggle, due to the deterioration of their material conditions of existence.

Chapter 5. The Decisive Turning Point

76 "Casa Gouveia (Empresa António Silva Gouveia, SARL), the representative of the CUF in Guinea, monopolized most of the commercial activities in the colony: import, export, shipping, and insurance. It was the oldest and most established company in the country. Projecting its activity both inside and outside the colony, Casa Gouveia spread commercial establishments throughout the territory and set up workshops, small factories, and shipyards in Bissau. For the circulation and flow of goods, it created a fleet that employed hundreds of sailors and dockers, all of whom were cruelly exploited.

As the holder of true power in Guinea through economic mechanisms, Gouveia was effectively the intermediary between overexploited Guinean producers and importers (be they Portuguese or foreign), whose interests it represented and defended." (Statement from the General Secretary, Aristides Pereira, at the symposium on "The Political Significance of the Pidjiguiti Massacre," Bissau, August 1 and 2, 1979. PAIGC Edition.)

77 Amílcar Cabral, Message of August 3, 1971.
78 See, attached, the excerpt from the statement made by the General Secretary of the PAIGC, Aristides Pereira, on the twentieth anniversary of the Pidjiguiti massacre.
79 Amílcar Cabral, Message of August 3, 1971.
80 At the end of a meeting held in Rome, on the sidelines of the Second Congress of Black Writers and Artists, in April 1959, Frantz Fanon and three MPLA leaders (Viriato Cruz, Lúcio Lara, and Mário de Andrade) agreed on the urgency of beginning the military preparation of Angolan militants in the foreign bases of the Algerian Liberation Army. Cabral was tasked with using one of his work trips to Angola to encourage the recruitment of young people there. The necessary contacts were established, but, for various reasons, the results of the recruitment drive were inconclusive. In the view of the Angolan forces, Frantz Fanon, Ambassador and Advisor on African Affairs to the National Liberation Front (FLN, Algeria) had, in 1960, and until his death, played a very controversial role vis-à-vis the support Angola deserved from the Algerian revolution. We reserve the opportunity, in another work, to definitively clarify the political and ideological divergence that pitted the MPLA against the celebrated author of *The Wretched of the Earth*.
81 *Palestras no seminário de quadros*, 1969.
82 See the text in the appendix. ["Abel Djassi" was Cabral's pseudonym, used during the clandestine phase of the liberation struggle.]
83 It adopted the acronym PAIGC on the occasion of the clandestine conference held in Dakar, from October 1 to 8, 1960, which decided on "the preparation for the final phase of the liquidation of Portuguese colonialism."
84 The party's forces were estimated and distributed as follows:
    a) the members (militants and sympathizers), around five thousand, were distributed in all regions of Guinea and in the main centers of the Cape Verde islands. Currently, the majority of members live in urban areas;
    b) the masses of all social strata belonging to the united front led by the party, the popular masses in general;
    c) elements organized abroad (Conakry, Dakar, and Ziguinchor). The main strength of the party was made up of workers in urban centers and peasant farmers (document published in Conakry on January 15, 1961 and signed by Amílcar Cabral and Aristides Pereira).
85 See the Memorandum to the Portuguese government. "*A prática revolucionária*," *Seara Nova*, 1977.
86 Unofficial response (of course) published in the newspaper *Novidades*, June 60/61.
87 Open letter to the Portuguese government. In "*A prática revolucionária*," *Seara Nova*, 1977.
88 Movimento Anti-Colonialista [Anti-Colonial Movement] (MAC), an organization created clandestinely in Lisbon in 1957 in the wake of the Consultation and Study Meeting for the Development of the Struggle Against Portuguese Colonialism" The definitive version of the MAC manifesto is dated January 1, 1960. (See: *O Militante*—organ of the CNG [National Council of Guinea] no. 11, January–February 1979, Bissau)
89 See: *A luta de libertação nacional nas colónias portuguesas: a conferência de Dar-es-Salam*, Algiers, 1967.

90 See: *Unidade e luta, I: A arma da teoria.* [Cited in the French version as *Unité et lutte, I: L'arme de la theorie*, op. cit., p. 75 and 106. We have included this here as it indicates the page from which the citation is taken, although from the French rather than the Portuguese, which is cited in the Portuguese version. *Unity & Struggle* is available in English published by Monthly Review, although that publication consists of only two-thirds of what was published in French.]

91 Ibid [p. 267 in the French].

92 An analogous program, in general terms, to that previously published by the MPLA.

93 See: *Unidade e luta, I: A arma da teoria*, op cit.

Part III. Sociology of People's War

Chapter 6. The People's War: A Model or a Path?

94 General Võ Nguyễn Giáp, *Guerre du peuple, Armée du peuple*, Maspero, 1966.

95 Ibid.

96 Nguyễn Khắc Viện, *Expériences vietnamiennes*, Editions Sociales, 1970.

97 Ibid.

Chapter 7. Emergence of the People's War

98 According to Cabral.

99 *Palestras no seminário de quadros, 1969.*

100 See: "As palavras de ordem," in *Unidade e luta, II: A prática revolucionária*, Ed. Seara Nova, Lisbon, 1976, Ch. 3, pp. 137–164. [*Unity & Struggle*, "General Watchwords," p. 224–251. This section in *Unity & Struggle* is a written summary of the Cassacá Congress by Cabral which was first published by the party in 1965, as mentioned by Andrade.]

Chapter 8. Viability of the Sociology of War

101 F. Constantinov, *Sociologia e ideologia: a sociologia na URSS. Relatório dos membros da delegação soviética ao VI Congresso Internacional de Sociologia*, Editions du Progrès, Moscow, 1966.

102 [See: Testimonies collected by Gérard Chaliand in *Armed Struggle in Africa: With the Guerrillas in "Portuguese" Guinea* published by Monthly Review Press.]

103 Cabral's pseudonym.

104 "Mensagem aos colonos portugueses na Guiné e Cabo Verde," in *Unidade e luta, II: A prática revolucionária*, p. 20. [*Unity & Struggle*, "Message to the Portuguese Settlers in Guinea and Cape Verde," p. 160–63]

105 "A batalha de Como e o Congresso de Cassacá," in *Unidade e luta, II: A prática revolucionária*, p. 43 [*Unity & Struggle*, "The Battle of Como and the Congress of Cassacá, p. 175–80].

106 *Palestras no seminário de quadros:* "Evolução e perspectivas da luta," 1969.

107 Ibid.

108 The VI conference of leading Party cadres, held in one of the liberated areas south of the Geba River [Cassacá], became the First Congress. See the newspaper *Libertação*, No. 39, February 1964.

109 *Palestras no seminário de quadros:* "Evolução e perspectivas da luta," 1969.

110 *Regulundade, catchorindade, mandjoandade* are all Guinean Creole terms.
111 *Palestras no seminário de quadros:* "Evolução e perspectivas da luta," 1969.
112 See: *Unidade e luta, II: A prática revolucionária,* Ch. 3, pp. 137–163 [In English, see *Unity & Struggle,* "General Watchwords," pp. 224–251. For the French, see: *Unité et lutte, II: La pratique révolutionnaire,* Ch. 3, pp. 188–223.]
113 At a few years' distance, Cabral had predicted the contradictions that, in the 1970s, emerged within the Portuguese colonial army and led to the captain's movement. [The "captain's movement" is the Armed Forces Movement, or MFA, which emerged in the Portuguese army and led the overthrow of the Salazar regime on the 25th of April, 1974. The rank of Captain in the Portuguese army was the highest which could be given to officers who were not brought up through the traditional military structure, but instead due to their having completed some level of higher education.]
114 One notes some degree of exaggeration in part of this statement regarding the loss of operational power of the enemy's war material in 1966 (see the chapter on the evolution of armed action and Cabral's military strategy).
115 See: "O Desenvolvimento da luta de libertação nacional na Guiné 'portuguesa' e nas ilhas de Cabo Verde em 1963", communiqué of January 17, 1964, in *Unidade e luta, II: A prática revolucionária.*
116 "As Palavras de ordem," ibid. [For English, see: *Unity & Struggle,* pp. 224–251.]
117 "A guerra de partisans e popular do movimento," ibid.
118 "Dez anos depois do massacre de Pidjiguiti," ibid.
119 "Intensifiquemos a luta em todos os planos da luta," ibid.
120 "A Situação da Luta do PAIGC em Janeiro de 1973"; ibid.
121 Lars Rudebek, a Swedish sociologist, provided a detailed description of the new social order emerging in the liberated regions in his book *Guinea-Bissau: A Study of Political Mobilization, Scandinavian Institute for African Studies,* Uppsala, 1974.
122 Currently [in 1980, ed.] general coordinator at the State Commissariat for National Education
123 *"As Palavras de ordem,"* in *Unidade e luta, II: A prática revolucionária. [Unity & Struggle,* 224–251.]
124 Currently [in 1980] Secretary General of the State Commission for Health and Social Affairs.
125 Currently [in 1980] State Commissioner for Economic Coordination and Planning.
126 *Afrique-Asie,* No. 66, September 23, 1974.
127 Today [in 1980] he is the State Commissioner for Justice.
128 Currently [in 1980] Executive Secretary of the CEL (Executive Committee of the War, equivalent to the Political Bureau) of the PAIGC.

Part IV. The Theoretical Contribution
Chapter 9. Imperialist Domination and the Driving Force of History

129 "Relatório geral sobre a luta de libertação nacional", in *Unidade e luta.*
130 See: Vladimir Ilyich Lenin, *Imperialism, the Highest Stage of Capitalism.*
131 If memory serves, this resolution was drafted by the ill-fated Moroccan leader Mehdi Ben Barka.

132 See: *Unidade e luta, II: A prática revolucionária*, Ch. 4: "As relações internacionais: as opções da CONCP," p. 165 [For English, see: *Unity & Struggle*, "The Options of CONCP," pp. 251–261].

133 Ibid., "A África e a luta de libertação nacional nas colónias portuguesas," p. 177.

134 [In colonial parlance, a "condominium" refers to a colonial territory shared by multiple colonial powers. Andrade is referring to the fact that multinational firms of many different nations operated widely across Portugal's African colonies.]

135 See: *Unidade e luta, I: A arma da teoria*, op cit. 7: "Fundamentos e objectivos da libertação nacional em relação com a estrutura social," pp. 199–213. [For English, see: *Unity & Struggle*, p. 119–138]

136 Ibid.

137 Ibid.

138 Ibid.

139 Karl Marx and Friedrich Engels, *The Communist Manifesto*.

140 Friedrich Engels, *Ludwig Feuerbach and the End of Classical German Philosophy*.

Chapter 10. The Social Lever of the Liberation Struggle

141 See: *Unidade e luta, I: A arma da teoria*, Ch. 4: "A estrutura social," pp. 101–116

142 Ibid.

143 Ibid

144 See: Yves Benot, *Idéologie des indépendances africaines*, Maspero, 1969.

145 See: Majhemout Diop, *Histoire des classes sociales dans l'Airiqae de l'Oues:* I. *Le Mali*, Maspero, 1971.

Chapter 11. The Role of Culture

146 The author presented these ideas in his speech at the Colloquium *"Cultura e de-senvolvimento, em Dacar, por ocasião do 70.o aniversário do Presidente Léopold Sédar Senghor,"* published in *Raízes*, No. 1, Praia, 1977.

147 See: *Unidade e Luta. I. A arma da teoria*. Ch. 8, "A cultura nacional," pp. 221–247.

148 Ibid.

149 Ibid.

150 Ibid.

151 Palestras no Seminário de Quadros, "Resistência cultural", 1969.

Appendices

152 In the French version published by Maspero, Andrade has an additional footnote about PIDE which reads *"Celle-ci n'était yas encore officiellement installée avec bureau et siège, mais elle était yrésente à travers les services d'administration et du coáunandement militaire* ("[PIDE] was not yet officially installed [in Bissau] with an office and headquarters, but [PIDE] was present [in Bissau] through its administration and military leadership").

Conclusion: The Current Place of Amílcar Cabral's Political Ideas

153 Theses for the Third Congress of the PAIGC, 1977.

154 "Palavras de ordem gerais," *Unidade e luta*.

155 Report to the Third PAIGC Congress, 1977.

Printed in the USA
CPSIA information can be obtained
at www.ICGtesting.com
CBHW031743260424
7528CB00004B/14